SECRET TALKS WITH MR. G.

To A Specially Formed Group
As Recollected by His Pupils

IDHHB,INC.
1978

Special thanks to the *Second Foundation.*

ISBN: 0-89556-001-1
Library of Congress Catalog Number: 78-54137

Note from the Editor

These talks are rememberances of conversations which occurred each day between G. and a special group formed in America for the purpose of insuring his obligation to future generations, as reported in several talks.

Even though these conversations are not direct transcriptions of his words, they are an authentic rendition of his ideas on work as they presented themselves during those times.

Even though he did not permit notes during his talks, a few students were able to reconstruct the essence of his talks, and without his knowledge made notes following the meetings. Later, these notes were compared, translations were made where necessary to the context and meaning, and tested in oral readings to many of those present when the talks were given.

Some passages were translated literally to give a sense of his idiomatic and informal use of language to express ideas. Some of these ideas may be new even to those who were present in his other groups, and some ideas may be shocking...But undeniably this record of his secret talks is one of the greatest contributions to date for those generations to come who wish to delve deeper than rumor and who demand to hear him actually voice his direct instructions to his pupils.

Contents

Contents

IV

V

Secret Talks With Mr. G.

Objective Magic

The result of my earlier researches was that I constated to myself the urgent necessity to further my understanding of ritual and its sub-study, what is called "magic". I do not mean by this the magic with which everyone is familiar, such as stage tricks or witchcraft. I concluded that there must be an older, more objective, magic about which those in the psychic and spiritualist trades knew nothing whatever.

I discovered through observation of my mediumistic companions that there were two widely divergent responses to the results of having broken the separating forces between cosmoses. Along with this I had constated to myself that only when describing the operation of laws of a higher cosmos manifesting in a lower cosmos could it be called objective magic.

To correctly separate the said two responses to results of higher forces proved difficult in the extreme because no one at that time had troubled to differentiate subjective and objective phenomena, and had instead classified them only in relation to results of ordinary life.

Thus there was then no objective science of phenomena just because the results and methods were completely identified with the reactions of people who somehow, usually mechanically and accidentally, managed to tap these higher forces for their own or their clients' benefit.

I was finally able to arrive at a working categorical understanding of the objective phenomena themselves, and decided to call those undertakings which required intentional action of higher centers — those centers which are properly the feeling and thinking centers, capable of emotional sensing and of mentation respectively, but which are ordinarily unformed through absorption of their rightful impressions by the false emotional and intellectual centers of the psyche — objective magic, having as its result the obtaining of real knowledge.

I thus separated this objective magic from its ordinary counterpart, "magic of the psyche,"in which purely fantastic results are obtained, and self-calming and amusement are the only attainments. Under this category I placed my former endeavors as a medium and psychic, as well as those results obtained by theosophy, occultism, and so forth, all of which up to then quite fascinated and attracted my attention. I had come to the point where I realized that something radically unexpected and important to my being had been hidden either intentionally or unintentionally behind all the other phenomena which were accessible to ordinary search by those individuals calling themselves psychics and mediums.

Up to that time I had focused on only those things which served my self-interests and those interests of my absolutely amusement-crazed clients, most of whom were exceedingly wealthy, who owing to the weakness of theirs to have everything go their own way all the time by exercising their power over others, were correspondingly bored. It was through the realization that all that I was doing for them at that time served no other purpose than to bring them momentarily out of their boredom and the resulting wish to be no longer just another means for alleviating their boredom that I was led to something deeper. This wish of mine to stop functioning as only one more short-term diversion for the rich led me to make a special vow with myself — the promise that I would at all costs find another way to use this extraordinary gift placed within me obviously not by myself or through my own efforts, since I had done nothing to discover or cultivate it, the means for psychometrizing objects having appeared in me spontaneously several years earlier — which vow took the form: "Never to live as ordinary beings live, and to discover regardless of the costs to myself, whether material or psychic, the real and objective use of my talent."

In understanding this special talent, I discovered that there were several underlying factors which, if understood in advance, would make possible the complete mastery of this method and its results far more rapidly than mastering one or two of its outer forms at a time. I had learned this when entering a monastery where certain movements were taught obligatorily in which one learned the combinations of these postures in group movements according to specific notations left by earlier generations of masters of their teaching. Had I but known beforehand that these odd and incomprehensible postures were nothing more than the persian alphabet in human body formations, and that the complicated dances were nothing more involved than the spelling of the chief aphorisms of the teaching letter by letter and sentence by sentence, it would have been simple to master them in one or two days just by learning the corresponding alphabet and matching one's posture to the sequence of letters in the aphorisms, providing one had them written out before one, as in fact they were, on cloth hanging from the ceiling around the teaching space, and to which the monks could refer if they lost their place in the sequence of movements. Upon learning this I broke out in a cold sweat when I recognized that there must be also an underlying factor behind all the phenomena I then called "objective ritual science" or objective magic, experiments in which I had been making since I was eleven years old, when thanks to accident or intention of other beings of whom I remain to this day completely unaware something intervened in my development, preventing the formation of the ordinary centers allowing instead the automatic completion of these centers in the essence by the removal of all obstacles for impressions, which as they reached these centers became substances which eventually crystallized in me and by themselves without any help from me formed with each other connections which provided a simultaneous experiencing in all centers and which at the same time — again without any action or effort on my part — provided me with the means to objectively mentate.

Through these same means it later became possible for me to influence the forms of the world in a real way and to call upon some beings which I now understand to be spiritualized and crystallized higher bodies of certain individuals who have completed themselves to the level of the solar system. I also mastered all sorts of odd skills usually thought of as occult, such as time and space travel in the sense of visiting through images — on many levels of being from the first throes of suffering of the primordial being to the reading of true history of the planet earth as well as many non-terrestrial histories, simultaneous tuning to objective thoughts proceeding through space and time, popularly called telepathy, making thought-forms, reading auras and other such phenomenal results of proceeding in higher cosmoses which appear unusual to ordinary senses and understanding.

Through all this it became obvious that it would be necessary in order to proceed, to destroy completely in myself all ordinary desires and interests, even those considered altruistic. This in turn led to a ruthless examination of all existing beliefs formed within myself about everything and everyone I had ever known or deduced for myself from second and third hand sources.

The result of this experiment with myself was crushing in

the extreme. I lost for many months any interest in going on in life, and succeeded in isolating myself totally from any experiential phenomena no matter how objective it seemed at the moment. In short, I lost contact with the universe, with myself, even with the source of all being. How I remained alive during this time is a mystery to me, because I remember nothing of any action taken to maintain my personal or physical existence. I may have gone for months without eating, drinking or sleep.

I discovered during this period of ruthless self-examination and purification from all existing current and previously recorded and crystallized beliefs that many of the images I had been receiving psychometrically were in fact nothing more than my own thoughts and beliefs triggered by objects and evironments. These all had to be firmly rooted out before any objective search could continue. At the same time I found the source of astral images, visions, formations of etheric images, microscosmic readings of the nervous system and cells of the human body, and other phenomena, apparently miraculous when viewed by ordinary man.

In this way I discovered quite by accident that all mystical states, trances and mediumistic abilities not just of my own arousal but also those of everyone I had known were no more than accidentally induced hysteria, even those concrete forms of vision associated with religious feeling and experience. In short, every experience of cosmos were projections triggered by one thing or another, having only an indirect foundation in reality.

I could not consider the existence of Objective Magic as established or true at this time, for I had no reliably objective data upon which to base such a conclusion. I was forced to put aside any conclusion and to simply proceed with the definite possibility that there might not be anything even remotely objective about anything beyond ordinary reality.

Moreover, in order to make an objective and impartial search for objective magic, I was forced to consider either result as an agreeable conclusion. It was also necessary to destroy within myself any vestige of prejudice regarding the outcome. Finally I was satisfied at least for the moment that I had arrived at the necessary state of impartiality.

I came to recognize that the method of unlocking mysteries related to psychometrizing sacred objects — shrines, artifacts, tombs and monuments might continue to be the most useful and effective means to the end I had already constated to myself — that of perfecting myself to the highest possible level beyond the natural perfection provided by nature itself, but that even this aim might change as my understanding unfolded.

My orthodoxy was shaken by the need to pursue this course of mine to unlock the secrets contained in various artifacts and moreover to accomplish this only through the means of psychometry. I discovered to my genuine fear that this form of search and the means to accomplish such an aim was viewed as unmistakably evil. Superstition surrounded the search, method, and objects themselves, some of which were not accessible by ordinary means due to the beliefs of those occupying the posts of guardians. In short, not only were extraordinary methods needed even to approach these sources of knowledge, but extreme secrecy was required of myself and of anyone associated with me in the search, otherwise unfortunate results could occur.

It became obvious to me then that something beyond mystical states and psychic phenomena which depended upon heightened emotional states might be aroused if one could separate the effect from mysticism accumulated during the past several millenia.

At the same time I understood that all manifestations of magic whether subjective or objective, are always associated with increased powers of emotion and greatly expanded scales of thought and perception, and cannot in any case occur without their simultaneous arousal, either naturally or artificially.

I understood that all religions no matter what their current form, had in the beginning the same founding cause and underlying factor — all stemming from one source which has kept itself hidden, but which issues periodically the means for the formation of new religions as they become necessary for the outer life of people and which serves as a guiding factor for the world at that time in history.

Even though accompanying "assisting factors" — incense, perfume, oils and powders — are perpetuated by existing religions, the use of active substances which serve to bypass the false emotional and intellectual centers has been suppressed. It was clear to me that in order to elevate the centers without false emotions, it would be necessary to avail myself of certain substances so contemptible and fearsome to modern man — although substances for the submergence of real and objective impressions and the activation of the mentating center are approved by him — for medical reasons only — and of the said approved pharmacology almost every contemporary being existing in the western world now partakes without understanding that these also are drugs. In accepting that these assisting substances were necessary to my aim, I resolved insofar as possible to keep such activities secret.

I had read somewhere or other about a sacred drink used in the Eleusinian Mysteries — and knew also of the inhalation of a special smoke used in the Delphic Mysteries. The use of these substances became imperative for me to personally elucidate. For this purpose it was impossible to ask anyone else about the subjective or objective nature of their own conclusions just because I had no way of determining impartially their real powers of objectivity in relation to experiments conducted by themselves upon themselves. In short, it became necessary to enact the anciently respected custom of performing experiments upon myself as the only available candidate who could be both subjective and objective and upon whose testimony I could determine exact reliability. That is to say, I was as a result of the need aroused by this aim of conducting self-experimentation both subjective and objective, forced to exterminate in myself all tendency to lie to myself about anything whatever.

This did not cause in me the expected suffering. It was of far more importance to settle once and for all some conclusive results of my madcap quest. In order to be done with it I resolved to suffer any little inconvenience, and made a promise to myself that when it was over I would return to my former life of ease and ignorance if I still desired it.

In connection with this promise I exacted the payment from my thoroughly angered self without any thought for the future use of these powers for self-amusement and aggrandizement to completely eliminate also all traces no matter how minute, of the tendency to invent excuses for my own actions, and to invent equally absurd historical events which proved to myself and to anyone who might be even only passively interested that I was not the fool I seemed to be at first.

It became necessary to first discover the exact active substances used by the ancients, knowing that the same substances would in all probability be the only ones that would unlock the secrets, as they were the same used to imprint them within the artifacts to begin with.

It was not only necessary to categorize these assisting substances according to the definite state induced, but also to associate with them the exact shrine, monument or artifact with which each had been used.

I was by this time aware of the properties of various substances used by the ancients, extracted from poppy, belladonna, datura stramonium, and hemp; their general applications, dosages and the body's capacity for their ingestion or for the ingestion of their smoke.

The uses of these substances in ancient and modern magic and alchemy is easily traced, as no secret is made of their employ, the writings of the various experimenters generally becoming available only after the cessation of their planetary form. No doubt remains to me of the wisdom of this course having already witnessed responses to release of such data.

Fortunately at that time I decided on an impulse proceeding in me from unknown causes either subjective or objective to undertake a journey just to acquaint myself with the necessities of wilderness survival and also not incidentally for the strengthening of my inner resources in dangerous situations.

Of course I knew that sacred gymnastics, asanas, dances, and movements could have certain similar effects to those induced by alkaloids, but these sometimes required more time, and the same results could usually — although not always — be obtained by the correct and careful use of active substances.

In my first experiments with toxic substances I made for myself three definite conditions; first that I learn whether or not an objective magic exists. Second, that I determine whether objective magic can exist separately from subjectivity. Third, that I discover a method of performing or arousing the said objective operations without any trace of sentimental associations. These early experiments clearly presented to me the near impossibility of such a series of aims.

The rapid change into completely unforeseen new forms caught me completely by surprise, and before I could stop myself I resisted the flow and became caught in the suffering of these new, for me, sensations.

This continued to plague me for nearly a year. I had very early understood that it was impossible to conduct such experiments too often due to their effects upon the nervous systems, and to the resulting automatic conditioning should one attempt this more frequently.

Not only did I encounter difficulties inherent in the use of these substances, but along with these came the problem that I had no language in which to express even to myself what I had learned.

Along with that I had still not learned to apply these substances to working with artifacts. Only later was I able to conduct these experiments in full force of public view without giving away to anyone what I was up to.

Aside from all this, the sense of separation which I had understood occurs to most people did not occur with me at all. Instead, I experienced an ingrowing, as if everything I was had become a single point, manifesting me in the most collected state possible. I noted that those with me on occasions when I involved myself with others during such experiments — were sometimes unable to recall their experiences, while I, on the contrary, was unable to forget even those things I would have preferred to allow to slip completely into oblivion if only for the sake of my inner peace and tranquility.

Through these experiments, I found myself within a special inner community quite invisible to ordinary people. Because of my new connection with this inner circle of humanity, I found a world which proceeds in an entirely different direction from the world known to ordinary man.

In these first experiments I was forced to learn that results could be totally unexpected. After a few such experiences it became obvious to me that I must not under any circumstances enter these states with any expectation whatever, nor limit my perception to the known or to the acceptable. I had to forgo any limits, emotional, perceptual or knowable that I had formed in myself or that had accidentally been formed in me through previous experience. I quickly recognized that any objective shock to the system could be used, provided it were safe enough to stop short — in some cases just exactly short — of total disruption of the life force in the body.

I toyed with the interchangeability of objective and subjective phenomena. I found that I could at will see either the astral, causal or material reality as real, automatically adjusting the other two realities to inventions of higher thoughts — a fiction in which I could become immersed if I wished to be.

In order to create and maintain these worlds it was necessary to crystallize thoughts in stabilized formations from simple to complex. This could only be accomplished by organizing all life force concentrations in relationships, each one of which I had been constrained to hold in place as a simple repeating cycle.

The important point for my realization at that time was not the exact relationship of one cosmos to another, but that I perceived directly now that everything in the universe was directly connected, and that moreover these forms were all connected just because they were all one and the same, repeated to provide the illusion of complexity. When presented with such a multiplicity of images, one can infuse them with differences sufficient to completely deceive oneself even though behind it all, one knows and understands the truth.

I knew during these times objectively without a single doubt that these experiences were real, and that the usual reality in which I lived from day to day was false. I resolved to remember myself, and to know always, and in every situation, that compared to that reality, ordinary reality is a dream.

When I had a companion or companions in these experiments we found that we could not communicate verbally in these spaces. Between words one could pass a lifetime. I realized that every word and every form in its turn has been the center of creation; it was almost impossible to remove oneself from the magnetic power of that word emanating to another cosmos in which another word was the Sun-Absolute. Each voyage seemed to me an eternity, beyond which nothing else existed. It surprised me, then, to see another word suddenly appear and at the same time see a whole new series of cosmoses expand from it to support it;

to make it real; to give it body and form to infinity — which same, incidentally, I could definitely perceive not too far away....

Another equally powerful effect of the use of these substances was that I could alter the flow of time at will. Soon, knowledge which came from these experiences was not sufficient. In short, I understood quickly that knowledge from experience is subjective and imaginary. It was in connection with my third sojourn that I encountered the abyss of infinity. Everything, as soon as it was formed, flowed into infinity in which it was transformed into the void and reformed as a new formation, which in turn was instantly swallowed.

I felt instant terror, and leaped up feeling at the same time that walking was impossible, as there was nothing upon which to stand. The abyss withdrew with a chuckling sound, making me wonder who was behind all the realities.

I came to realize that it would be impossible to move beyond my present understanding without crossing that abyss, and so resolved to allow myself to be drawn through it to the other side. A death was required for each resurrection.

Coming back through the now familiar world of triads which in their absolute simplicity make up all forms of complexity, I discovered placed within the dream of ordinary life certain "landmarks" which I could now see quite clearly for the first time, and which I knew I would have to visit in order to obtain from them the knowledge which had been placed in the crystallized world for safe-keeping.

It was in this way that I constated to myself that in the world there were forms which were "Holders of Knowledge" which could be tapped intentionally, if I only knew how to release them. But I also knew that these were not remembered by modern civilizations, and that in order to locate them and read them it was necessary to somehow obtain a map of the ancient world which contained an accurate description and location of the anciently existing monuments, artifacts and shrines.

I could feel the specific moods of old objects in particular, and it was in this state that I encountered either accidentally or through intervention of higher — I hope higher — forces, an ancient monument. Through this monument which I accidentally tapped by the use of certain active substances in collaboration with a few words of antiquity, I learned the secret of relation of the two great cosmic laws.

The emotional impact of receiving data from objects which were in themselves sentient beings was enormous on my own presence. It was as if I had never existed except to perceive and appreciate in their absolute states everything about themselves.

At this same time I found within my own form many separate entities, each with its own life, thoughts, attitudes and needs, and with whom it became possible for me to communicate, although not in the ordinary conversational way.

I saw also through the medium of this giant dolmen a geometric form deep within it, which formed a sphere with nine planes intersecting it at intervals. These planes continually folded in on each other and on themselves, creating the effect of a lotus collapsing inward upon itself. I understood at once that this was the form of the living world, and that should I somehow prematurely penetrate beyond this formation, it would cause my annihilation just as surely as would absorption into infinity.

Mastering the animal

Information can be transmitted to anyone, but knowledge only to family, from father to son.

The notes which fill in the "mi-fa" and "si-do" intervals do not exist on the same octave. To traverse the interval one must borrow from a different octave.

The first interval occurs just as one enters the Work. It is the "work wishing" — to wish for something more than life. Dissatisfaction is the result of many years of immersion in life and the final realization that nothing offered in life is worth anything in itself.

Work wishing must enter from another octave of influence. This is the first "mi-fa" interval of the school. Here for new candidates there is only one percent work wish as contrasted to ninety-nine percent personal wish. Some people have at this stage only a whim, others a real necessity.

If the work wish becomes activated, one can work regularly without outside help until the "si-do" interval, at which time another outside shock must be provided in order for one to continue.

The "si-do" interval is that period of work on oneself in which one comes face to face with one's chief feature, or animal. During this moment of recognition it is necessary for the animal to become aware of your interest to make rapid progress past this point absolutely essential. If one remains passive the animal will emerge the victor.

Once the animal is aware of your activities it is only a matter of a very short time before it will begin to struggle for its continued life without mercy and completely ruthlessly.

When you and the animal come face to face it is like two adversaries seeing each other for the first time. Along with this shock of recognition there is for both of you a real smell of danger. When this occurs you must immediately begin to fight for your life, because you have at the most only three months before you master the animal or it becomes master.

It can only be mastered if it does not know that it is being mastered. If it becomes aware of these intentional activities of yours, it will by all means remove itself from the source of irritation — which in this case is the school.

There are schools which teach the animal to overcome essence. The pupils of such schools are highly imaginative in explaining to themselves and others the reasons for their self-love.

The introduction of these ideas is sufficient to precipitate this struggle. Just hearing these ideas without acting upon them can bring one closer to the point of recognition.

It is dangerous to arrive at the point-of-recognition when one is not prepared, does not have real techniques, and cannot get help and data for mastering the animal.

To get the attention of the animal when one wishes to activate this struggle, one must summon the animal with knowledge. In the old sense conjure means "with knowledge."

If one can converse with one's own animal, one can speak with any animal, for all two-brained and one-brained animal languages are the same. This is the real meaning of the story of St.Francis of Assisi who knew how to talk with the animals and to master them with love. It is even possible to do this with wild animals eventually.

To make the animal obey, one must begin with small things. The development of a special inner will starts in the moving center. If you know how to do in one center, it gives clues necessary for work in directing attention of all centers.

The battle to master the animal is like angel and devil. What was once heaven for you and which said place you wished formerly to keep as quiet and calm as possible now becomes a field upon which a series of pitched battles ensues. This struggle is a function of being. It is not something one can decide to do or not to do.

Compare this to the situation of a burglar locked inside a safe accompanied involuntarily by a bomb which is preset to explode at an unknown time. The bomb cannot be reached and the fuse and timer cannot be dismantled until he opens the safe. He does not know the combination of the safe but he has all his burglar's tools and knowledge of safes and locks. He must work quickly and effectively. At the same time he must not think even once of the possible consequences while working to release himself from this situation. If even for a moment he loses himself it could have been the crucial time he otherwise needed. Perhaps the margin of error is only one moment. In this case the bomb explodes and he is killed. Although he must work under extreme pressure, he must not allow tensions to interfere with his skills. This is exactly how you must work with the animal in order to master it. You must become in every respect a professional.

Various factors in mastery of the animal become important where they were not important before. To begin with, one must be very cunning. In this way, one can exact promises from the animal in exchange for little things — but these little concessions must be harmless; and if possible, whimsical.

For instance, one can allow the animal to "go to the zoo for one day" in return for making a funny face in front of everyone. One must offer something harmless but interesting to the animal in exchange for something small the animal would not mind doing as a task to pay.

If you cannot think immediately of a way for the animal to pay, you must not do this. Only with a definite exchange is this technique genuinely effective. This method is called *bargaining factor.*

After the promise has been extracted the animal is given its reward. This is the *reward factor.* The animal should not be totally satisfied, but the reward must not be denied. The animal gets very angry and lashes back dangerously.

In order to bargain with the animal, one must know very well what the animal wants.

Any aid used in making bargains with the animal is called an *assisting factor.* It may be Armagnac, cigarette, Turkish coffee. It takes experience to be able to use *assisting factors.* One must get the animal pleasantly tipsy without getting drunk oneself.

Study to find the *vulnerability factor* of the animal. However, you must hide your own vulnerability.

In bargaining with the animal, you must know when you are able to say "no" and when you are not. If you try to stop the animal and you allow it to disobey, even one time, it will never obey you again. It will not take you seriously. You must say "no" only when you have will to enforce "no."

II

Clubs of a different kind

It is necessary that you work in order to maintain planetary existence. At the same time you have many responsibilities toward people; mental, emotional, and physical. During these times, you cannot really be bothered with thinking about something. I do not suggest that you think about these questions at all. I give you techniques of this. It is so simple that perhaps it was overlooked.

To mentate means temporarily, at least, to make a question center of gravity. Everything you do in life, no matter how ordinary is done only in relation to that question as center of gravity. That question becomes for you your inner God, replacing inner evil God at least temporarily.

My question which for years became my all-independent-parts-taken-together center of gravity, was at first consciously initiated, and then by inertia proceeded. "Is it true that God suffers?" Everything I did in relation to this question. To make a center of gravity you must also give time limit. This creates sense of urgency.

[23]

When I make a question center of gravity, I do this with my whole being. After working with my first groups, I discovered that most were not able to do this at all. This is because they could not make a question of life and death, even in play.

When I saw the group in New York, I made the serious discovery that there were people who behaved quite unbecomingly, in spite of the fact that they were outwardly at least interested in my ideas. This question has become for now my center of gravity. Years ago I had the gravity center question, "How is it possible to help individuals to exterminate in themselves the tendency towards suggestibility?" At the same time I also realized that they had no center of gravity of their own, and therefore could not make a center of gravity for themselves. Suggestibility means to take whatever center of gravity presents itself from moment to moment. I developed a means to make it possible for an individual to eradicate in himself this suggestibility. But to do this requires at least some effort. Effort requires some interest. Interest requires that questions be important. I discovered that people are quite happy the way they are. So then I was forced to wait for beings dissatisfied with ordinary life and what it could provide.

For a long time I believed that only such individuals would come to me to work. Then I discovered that some could be quite satisfied with life and yet come to a school.

By every means possible it becomes necessary now to enact whatever is required to make it possible for only those who are interested in work to come here and to remain here. I find that even stepping on corns does not work. That people *like* corns to be stepped on.

S: I have wondered about that same thing and I have noticed one thing, I do not know if it will shed any light on it. Sometimes when I am talking to people about the ideas, they feel obligated somehow to stick with it even though they have no actual interest in working. There is some sort of conditioning to study an idea that comes along that is more powerful, more all-encompassing, than any one you have heard before.

G: Still, a certain amount of this is to be expected. For individuals to come here just to sit at table and smell food, but not to eat food, what can I do? To not eat food is disrespect.

S: Apparently some people simply sit waiting for more ideas. As you say, they come not to work with them but to smell them.

G: You must understand that all my ideas as presented to you are "third food shit."

S: People will come to hear your ideas and at first will get some satisfaction from them, then after a while become miserable and apathetic — yet feel obliged to remain.

G: They find the school is not what they thought it was.

S: And yet feel a great reluctance to leave, and are not really here.

G: If these ideas could be presented beforehand, before they come directly under my influence, then perhaps they never come. They find that they cannot work with these ideas, that they only come to sniff ideas.

S: It has to be also a slight taste of what is required.

G: Then this is responsibility of study group leaders.

S: But also, perhaps, if we are in the situation here where people are already present at the school, that perhaps there should be a study group set up even here.

G: In England and America, is possible to set up study groups.

P: Seems to me that people have conditioning which tells them to seek the highest ideas that they can. When they get here, they come in contact with a higher level of work than they have been able to come in contact with before.

Because of this conditioning it may be necessary to send those people away, and give them something specific to do so that they do not feel that they have failed in their task. There is no place within themselves where they can make the decision necessary for them to leave.

G: If I send them away, this makes external obstacle as well as internal obstacle. They not only have to overcome this in themselves, but also the obstacle which I placed in them by sending them away. Better to have study group leaders who are able to take responsibility. Then if they do not like it, I never see them. If once they come to my table, I am forced to offer hospitality. To refuse hospitality is a big sin.

P: The difficulty is that if those people have the possibility of doing work as study group leaders, they are also likely to be people who have the possibility of making use, in a real way of your presence.

G: I do not wish for you to become identified with me, but with my ideas. This is a dilemma that I have realized for many years.

S: If those in the work group are working intensely with the ideas, perhaps our demanding of others the same thing would provide the sifting process that is needed. I am starting to feel more and more like being more and more outwardly prodding.

G: You must take into account how much time I have to work with you. Also, I have a great many other things which I am forced to do which have no relation at all to you. During those times it is not possible for me to work with you. I only have a limited amount of time to prepare you as candidates, and also as preparers of candidates. I see now that all other groups as it stands now are even though perhaps able to prepare themselves, definitely not able to prepare others. You come to my work recently. They came earlier. When they came certain things were done. Today these things are no longer productive. Yet they will not allow for my understanding to change. Therefore they continue only in way with which they are already familiar. You on the other hand as a group have no preconceptions about this. An entirely new way to work must be found — a way to work for the future. In short, I must develop with this group, a way to work which is changeable to the situation. I find that I must teach you not to preserve things with nothing added and nothing taken away, but to add and take away as necessary. In short, to teach you how to make work. External manifestation is necessary, always necessary. But this can be anything. It can depend on many factors. To understand underlying factor, is to have the means to make work for any given situation. One possibility is for the work group to encapsulate itself during its work, and then each day work with a study group — or maybe many study groups. But this demands of you that you learn to work as I do. For instance, you must be able not only to give group work, but also individual work. You must be able to correct an individual in direction. You must also learn, as I did, although not in the same way that I learned it, to provide "enabling factor"— Seed for soul.

P: Is it possible to provide this enabling factor before one has taken on an obligation which brings us under the law of the work?

G: Perhaps. I do not know. I do not see how it is possible.

P: Yet if one is under the obligation to the Work then that will be given.

G: The means is provided. However — on what scale? This is the question. If one wishes for a higher scale, one must make efforts to take greater obligation. To take greater obligation, one must learn how to become necessary. For my center of gravity at this moment, these are all questions which are not necessary.

   The question which becomes necessary is simply how to make impossible the continued presence of those individuals who come only to sniff "higher turd".

V: Disguise it as chocolate, everyone likes chocolate.

G: Already disguised as chocolate. Food at my table is unrecognized higher ideas.

P: Have you tried requiring of people before they come into the work space to come with a question?

G: They do not make question their center of gravity. How can there be results? They come with question to make conversation, as "ticket to table."

P: Then if a question comes as a ticket or as a conversation piece and they were told, "No, that does not get you in..."

G: Then, my home becomes restaurant. If I sit at cafe, and someone comes to my table to ask question and question is not gravity-center question, then I can refuse. But in my home I cannot refuse.

P: Even after three days you cannot establish conditions?

G: No, because still turns home into restaurant. Perhaps only meet people in cafe. I think already it is too late turn my home into restaurant. Enabling factor for this only grows in America, and does not come to me in sufficient quantity to make restaurant. But possibility for you, to make restaurant where everyone must pay for entrance with center of gravity question. But if commercial enterprise, must be entirely commercial. Everything must be paid for, with money, with center of gravity question, with service and effort. I try to bury dog so to make attention necessary. But people can still come and never pay attention. In special clubs, where everything must be paid for, laws of hospitality do not apply. This is why I have idea of clubs. Perhaps years after my death, these clubs will finally begin to operate. In any case, those power-possessing beings who have enabling factor for greasing wheels of commercial enterprises, which have as their principal place of formation America, do not now wish to release any of these substances for my work. So I have position like Moses. I can see across Jordan, but I myself will never arrive.

You must find a way to open these clubs, and make entirely commercial. Eradicate in the club, but not in your home, all traces of hospitality. Make entirely commercial. Make it so that everything must be paid for. Of those who come to clubs, perhaps there are some that you wish to invite to your home. But if once invited to your home, you must always give hospitality no matter what. So you must be careful who you invite to home after club. I suggest to make like businessmen's club. In this way, is possible to make everyone pay for everything. I hope before I die to give you everything necessary to make possible such clubs. In any

case, those with whom I have been working in the past,
would not make such clubs. I cannot even tell them this idea.
They already have habit to make everything hospitality. If
such clubs fall under law of hospitality, it would be complete
failure.

Also, along with this, I hope to give you special indications
what to do with results of commercial enterprise. To go on
spree, must earn everything for yourself. Money derived
from work only can rightly be used for work. To propagate
ideas, keep club alive.

You cannot expect help from those who have been with me
for a long time. They will reject these ideas. They will even
reject you, and believe you to be upstarts. I am sure of this.
Their work already is crystallized. They cannot break down
this crystallization. Perhaps what they do also will be useful.
In any case, they can never open clubs of a different kind.
Impossible for them. They are not sufficiently mercenary.
They wish only to give what they have received in the same
way they have received it.

It may be a long time before power-possessing beings are
willing to help with vast amounts of ordinary currency
needed. But then maybe you will have grown old. Only your
children perhaps can do this. Everything depends upon
power-possessing beings, who usually do not wish to lend
their efforts in these directions. If they do, they wish to
receive some benefit for it, but they cannot receive benefit
because they are aristocracy. If they start as prince, give
everything to the work, and become like pauper, only then is
something possible for them. They remain aristocracy
because they are afraid.

Even those who have been with me for many years know
nothing of special clubs which I make now. I see now that
greater scale must be in terms of number of clubs; that each
individual club must by itself be on small scale. Almost
completely necessary for these to be restaurant. Very similar
to businessmen's clubs, only businessmen's clubs for both

men and women.

Perhaps each club can contain gymnasium, even steam bath. To do this would take a great many American dollars. No one here has this in sufficient quantity to do anything real. Maybe by next year, I can shear some sheep.

But I am feeling very tired these days. Perhaps this is a signal that for me, the work is ended. If this is the case, then you must first learn to use, and only then, make these ideas public. Of course they will "deny you like Peter." It becomes necessary for many years to pass before announcement and commencement of these clubs. Possibly by then, no one even interested. May be no hunger in world by then. Also, perhaps, everyone unable to accept new form.

In any case, I see as our task now to increase necessity for these clubs, to make for you understanding how to run these clubs, so that both work and preparation for work can be accomplished in the same club. One such club is not sufficient. Even two or three clubs is not sufficient. There must be at least twenty-four such clubs opened simultaneously in every major center of civilization. This means somewhere you must find a way to shear not only one, but many millionaires.

J:　We must then be shown data for running these clubs in a specific way, to provide possibility for candidates to develop.

G:　My drones can teach how to operate club. You be my drones to teach other factors. To run club outwardly I already prepare many such people. To run club inwardly, I prepare your special group.

Each day a new national gravity-center dish must be prepared. Unlike in my home, this must be paid for in currency. Also unlike in home, everyone who comes to club must have ticket every day. All members of the club must pay for its existence in every way possible. Who works in club must be paid in whichever way they wish. Those who wait on table, those who are steam bath attendants, must be paid for in exact amount necessary to make those individuals self-supporting.

In commercial club, everything must pay for itself. In one month, maybe less, I can teach you how to do this. It now is January. By March you will be able, but after that your efforts must be directed toward understanding method of opening and maintaining club. One-third effort must be toward maintaining and developing fully, inner knowledge. But...along with this, necessary to seek power possessing beings and convince them of necessity for such clubs. This may take twenty, thirty, forty years, even more, perhaps.

But you must be on watch for one who is to come, who can direct all this. Not resist when this work is taken by one who is being prepared now to take my work. He must have a friend inside the work. I know in my earlier groups they will not accept him. I will later tell you certain signs by which you will know him when he comes. Only he who is prepared specially for director and organizer of my work in future will have these manifestations.

The animal is
law-conformable

Obligation to the Work is enabling force to make choices on objective basis rather than on random whim or what the animal wants. How can we be sure that these are from beneficent higher sources, rather than disguised impulses which the animal has made to misdirect us? Knowledge of the animal is necessary because all the animal's actions are law-conformable.

M: What I wanted to clarify was that if we have insight about what the animal does, we would be able to know something coming from the animal.

G: You are trying to think about this in ordinary terms. You say if it does the same thing every time then predictability can be ascertained. The fact is, the animal does not do the same thing every time. You do not understand the meaning of 'law-conformable.'

S: When P. said that, I got the impression that the responses the animal would make would be knowable, because it would follow a certain pattern, if you knew the law. I do not know what that is.

G: Therefore, what position are you in exactly, relative to self-study?

M: How can you recognize whether an influence comes from the animal or not?

G: The actions of the animal are law-conformable.

P: The resultant action can come about from a moving center, emotional center or intellectual center influence.

G: Action is the result of behavior.

P: That is the manifestation.

G: And what is the primary cause of behavior?

P: Law.

G: Which set of laws are operant to result in behavior?

P: That is the point. Behavior is law-conformable. There is a certain set of laws of the animal in nature, the world that the laws come from, that the animal is held under.

G: And how would you characterize this world, in which these laws exist, and from which these laws operate? Is it the same world in which the animal exists, or is it quite a different world altogether, in which these laws originate and are crystallized?

P: It is a different world.

G: Are these laws in fact crystallized in the world of origin?

P: No. There is an octave.

G: There is an octave. Is there any world of crystallization of those laws? Are these laws objective or subjective laws?

P: Objective.

G: So they are objectively crystallized in some space.

P: Yes.

G: What is the force through which these are connected?

P: Through the planetary body.

G: And what happens to this connection when the body dies, or is transcended?

P: It is redeemed.

G: Under ordinary circumstances the animal must conform to these laws.

P: True.

G: Does this set of laws pertain to only certain kinds of animals, or to all animals in general?

P: All animals everywhere.

G: Can it be said to also pertain to all life everywhere, or do we differentiate life from animal?

P: It is pertaining to all life.

G: Does it also pertain to all forms everywhere?

P: Yes.

G: This set of laws you say is operant for all forms. Therefore, could you differentiate for me why we would talk about different laws for mineral and for animal. I already know what I am looking for. I ask a question in a particular way to force a particular answer.

In what way does this set of laws differ in relation to its action upon various kinds of forms?

P: There are fewer degrees of freedom in the set of laws governing the mineral, and progressively more degrees of freedom as we go to the vegetable and the animal.

G: How do you know this to be true?

P: I see it.

G: How objective and reliable is your perception? Surely it is more than you see. You have been told this by someone.

P: It passes other tests. It is consistent. Also I have verified it from study.

G: Obviously this formulation of ideas is something which was not your own, which you tested.

P: Correct.

G: And you found your test satisfactory.

P: Yes.

F: If this has happened, then it seems as though the mineral world somehow happened by gradually taking away some freedom of which the world above it might have more.

G: Has freedom been taken away, or have laws been

added?

F: That is what I was wondering. If laws are added, does that take away from the freedom that was there before?

G: Is there a relationship to the number of laws to which something is subject, and the amount of freedom which it enjoys?

P: Yes. The fewer laws, the greater freedom, but also the greater need to follow the laws.

G: The fewer laws, the more law-conformable.

P: If something were subject to only one law, it would be absolutely law-conformable.

G: You say the higher the scale, the fewer the laws, greater the freedom. At the same time, the more law-conformable one becomes. So one is freer to some extent, and yet as one obeys fewer laws, one obeys them more firmly. Another factor must be introduced, called inexactitude.

P: At the moment I think it comes about because as there are more laws, there is a greater possibility of them coming into conflict with each other.

G: Therefore, one could be subject to one law, and then change subjection to a different law. One is subject to fewer influences higher up on the scale; one has fewer choices of influence, whereas lower on the scale one can switch from one influence to another, although one is conforming to each influence law-conformably.

P: That is how it seems.

G: So the inexactitude is in terms of transfer of influence. Is that so?

P: Yes, particularly at that interval ''transfer of influence.''

G: And also during that transfer, one would have, momentarily at least, a certain freedom to move from one cosmos to another. How much more law-conformable is the vegetable than the mineral?

P: Somewhat more than twice as much.

G: Animal behavior is law-conformable. How many fewer laws in the animal world than in the vegetable world?

P: Half as many.

G: Notice that for the moment we are ignoring worlds on greater scale. We can also assume from what you say that the animal kingdom contains the vegetable kingdom and that the vegetable kingdom in turn contains the mineral kingdom. Is this so?

P: Yes.

G: In your opinion are these various worlds connected by class? Do they contain each other, or are they separate?

F: No, they are not separate.

G: Then how are they related? For example, how are the animal kingdom and the vegetable kingdom related?

F: There is a continuum of laws.

G: Good. There is also an additional set of laws equal to the set of laws to which the animal is subject.

F: So we cannot really say that the animal contains the vegetable.

G: There is twice the number, but they are totally different laws?

F: They are not different.

G: Then how would we find the laws in the animal that are also in the vegetable? Would we not find half of the vegetable kingdom laws equivalent to the full laws in the animal kingdom?

F: Yes.

G: In order to use those laws, do we have to know all those laws specifically, or is there a set of laws that is knowable which we could apply in order to derive these laws at need?

F: We could derive them at need.

G: How many laws are necessary to know in the animal world in order to observe, study, understand, and work with the animal?

P: One law.

G: I am assuming that we need to know the laws of the animal kingdom to work with the animal. Is this true?

P: Yes, to work precisely.

G: Therefore, I would have more efficiency, would I not? If as an example, we threw away all laws that pertain only to the plant and mineral kingdoms, I would have a more efficient working basis.

P: Inasmuch as work with the animal is in relationship with the Work.⌐

G: I am now dissociating figure from ground, isolating the figure itself. The animal not in relation to its environment, but only in relation to itself. I am differentiating essence and being.

P: We do not need other sets of laws to work with the animal?

G: We can assume that we will need further knowledge of laws of environment, as well as laws of animal. Is this true?

P: Yes.

G: We can assume it is not necessary to memorize all laws.

P: That would be impossible!

M: Is it necessary to have mastery over the animal in order to identify whether an influence comes from the animal or from somewhere else?

G: Would you define what you mean by "somewhere else"?

M: Higher sources.

P: If by mastery you mean the ability to manipulate the animal, no. But we do need understanding.

G: I wish to know more about law-conformableness. In

passing, I would also like to elucidate another question. You say that the behavior of the animal is law-conformable. Always law-conformable?

P: Yes.

G: To what laws must the animal conform?

P: The laws of the animal world.

G: Is it possible that it must also conform to laws below the animal world under certain circumstances?

P: Yes.

G: Under what circumstances could it fall under influence of lower world laws?

P: Under the same circumstances that a human could fall under the laws of the animal world.

G: So a human, then, is subject to different laws than an animal. We make differentiation between human and animal. I put that aside for a moment. What conditions could cause an animal to become subject to the laws of plant or the laws of mineral?

F: I do not think that it actually can be subject to those laws, but it can act as if it is.

G: Aha! What would cause behavior as if subject to laws not normally subject?

F: If it was jumping between laws quickly and there was pressure on it from somewhere.

G: Why would it be jumping from law to law?

F: If we observe the animal in action it might feel trapped.

G: We now have an intuitive insight through which we can ask questions on scales larger than we could before. Therefore, I must now ask you: is it possible for an animal to become subject to laws above itself, above its world, to which it would not ordinarily be subject, as well as to worlds below itself?

P: Yes.

G: Without asking particularly how it would occur, if subject to, in lower kingdoms, would then seek higher kingdoms of laws to become subject.

P: That is not the only way it could happen.

G: What are you thinking of?

P: I am thinking of the way in which, in this particular case, we could bring the animal under the set of laws it is subject to.

G: How could we do this?

P: Redemption.

G: What is the active of redemption?

P: Something done from higher to lower.

G: And where does it form actively?

P: In the higher.

G: In which higher, specifically?

P: It has to formulate from each scale above.

G: If it stops where it becomes passive, why is it not also passive in the lower kingdom? If you understand what is being asked, you have practical knowledge how to deal with the animal. Then I must ask you this: You say only one law is necessary to know, in order to derive all laws to which the animal is subject.

F: You would need one law, but you also would need a law to know how to derive.

G: So you need a basic law, and then you need a deriving law. How many deriving laws are necessary?

P: Two.

G: Are any other laws necessary besides those in order to derive laws for any particular world, or does this apply to any world?

P: The second law can be derived from the first.

G: Under what circumstances could that law be transmitted?

F: When there is a receptive for it, in states where it was known. When it was able to make a receptive.

G: How could we eliminate conditioning and expectation in order to make ourselves receptive to the formulation of this law?

F: I do not know.

G: Let us see if we can find out. P. obviously knows some laws. For purposes of this discussion say I know nothing of any of these three laws. I choose to call the first law that we called attention to, the *Great Law*. Do you understand what I mean when I say the *Great Law*?

P: Yes.

G: Then the second law is the first law of derivation. The third law, which is the law of direct application, I would choose to call the *Law of Movement*. The first law we can call the *Law of Triads,* and the second law we can call the *Law of Ninefoldness.* Is this correct in your formulations?

F: It is the law of deriving other triads from the original.

G: And what steps does this follow?

F: It seems that there is a triangulation that happens which gives a point of leverage, and from that one, another one can be reflected.

G: I will leave, for the moment, the processes of restorials and derivation. Are there any other laws we need to know about?

F: We can probably do with those for now.

J: Do these three laws operate in particular in relationship to understanding the law-conformability of the animal?

G: Yes. But we learned something else. Man is slightly above animal on this scale.

F: What do you mean by scale?

G: Man is subject to fewer laws than the animal, is this true?

F: Yes, the real human.

G: The real human. Ah! Wait, wait, wait...Is there also false human?

F: Yes.

G: And in what world does the false human live?

F: Every world.

G: All worlds. So the false human is as if subject to *all* laws.

F: Yes.

G: Is there also a false animal?

F: No.

G: So only third brain makes possibility of false human. False human is potentially subject to all laws. So there is a human world which is higher than the animal world in the scale we are using. The human world then is for real humans, half the laws of the animal world. Is this true or is there another world between those?

F: No, that is it.

G: Can I then infer that there is a membrane between certain worlds?

F: Yes.

G: Is there a higher world than the human world, in terms of fewer laws?

F: Yes.

G: Which world is that called?

F: The spirit world.

G: Is there between plant and animal also such a membrane? Or is it not necessary?

F: I do not think it is necessary.

G: So then higher than the angel world, there is still another world. Is there a membrane in between those worlds, and also between each succeeding world?

F: No.

G: No? Only lower than man and higher than man?

F: Yes.

G: We have then elucidated the source of beneficence, the reliability, and the objectivity. I could not possibly ask these questions unless I knew already what we were looking for. If you are extremely receptive you then immediately begin to put higher influences into active condition. Truth, P., it is an active thing you do, but still in a receptive state. How could you then determine reliability and objectivity? Let us take them one at a time. To begin with, are laws from an unknown source?

P: Yes.

G: You say there are only three laws you need. Using those three laws, can you guess at source?

P: Yes. Although it is new to me, a law is always conformable.

Obligation and
law of octaves

Madame: The possibility of in ordinary life supplying our own shocks in order to continue work on ourselves depends, as I see it, upon the ability to understand the conditions which exist in nature. We react to these without attention to the mechanics, chemistry or mathematics of the octave. One who understands the law of octaves is able to see the mechanics of ordinary life, thus it is possible to supply our own shocks only then. To self-apply these small shocks we do not require a teacher, but in the beginning we are completely dependent on him until we learn to do for ourselves what he does for us. In this respect the work on ourselves is tailor-made and no general rules apply to everyone.

T: Because we do not know how to get into a higher octave, we continue to repeat the old one.

Madame: Yes. In ordinary life we repeat the same octave over and over again because we do not understand the mechanical laws under which we are forced to live.

G: In order to introduce a new octave we must have two

octaves from which we can borrow notes. Before we are able to do this, we must first accept the existence of the interval. For instance, P. has something he wishes to say. He gives himself ten minutes in which to say it. If he does not manage to say everything in this period of time, he feels he may forget what he intended to say, because he knows that another "I" will represent his presence by then. Because he does not wish to be interrupted at all during this time, he does not pay attention, and misses both intervals. Thus he returns automatically to his starting point "do" once again, having gone nowhere. Had he seen the necessity to introduce notes in place of the intervals, he would have allowed someone else to introduce subjects entirely different than the subject of his talk at those points...of course in his estimation the worst points possible...and thus completing the octave on a new level higher than the original octave. Because he is a vain man he does not use notes supplied to him by outside influences. This is why during toast I provide missing notes. Master of ceremony is responsible for integrity of the original octave, but I am responsible for introduction of peculiarities from other octaves...lawful inexactitudes.

Madame: For ordinary man there is a feeling that in order to present an idea conforming to his idea of himself he must first start at "do," work completely around, and end up at "do" again. What seems to happen as I see it is that the impressions are not really getting to other individuals. It is not being digested, because it does not have added to it food from a higher octave. Ordinary man hears only his own echo.

G: Truth. For him there is no possibility of communicating ideas. For ordinary man there is no possibility of communicating because he speaks from the wrong center and does not allow the octave to proceed consciously. He speaks to the false centers. To speak to real centers is only possible if octave has borrowed notes filling the intervals.

Introduction of peculiar notes is not supplied in nature. They must be supplied consciously, but to do this one must be able to see the octave in complete form. One must realize that one has come to an interval, one must see the note which needs to be supplied, one must supply the missing note, and then proceed. In order to crystallize an octave into its complete form, however, one must complete at least one more interval. For instance, P. has difficulty baking bread because he does not know certain things. He sees B. baking bread. He sees everything that B. does, but B. knows details. B. has not only the great octave of baking bread, but also small octaves within baking bread.

Madame: He is more aware of subtleties.

G: He has not only the major chord, but he also has harmonica. Within each octave are many small octaves. For instance, you supplied a note when you spoke just then. The thing you supply is a note, but the note is also a complete octave in itself. This octave also requires two additional external shocks in order to complete itself. Each of those shocks is an octave in itself and requires two additional shocks for its completion. Reconciling forces in this case constitute an entire octave.

The borrowed octave is quite different from the action one may be taking. Therefore it is rejected by ordinary man. For instance, P. is talking about bread. In order to bake bread, certain things are necessary. He wishes to talk about these things. Then, suddenly, Madame talks about a sport. P. does not wish to speak about a sport. He wishes to speak about bread. Therefore he rejects the note supplied by the borrowed octave. This of course can only be the introduction of the "do" of that borrowed octave, not the complete octave itself. Perhaps he is interested in that sport. Then instead of refusing it, he leaves the octave of baking bread, and goes to the sport octave, and becomes identified with it. Now completely captivated, he falls under the influence of the octave which was only intended to supply a shock to the octave he wishes not only to complete, but also to bring to a higher scale.

Let us call one of these missing notes X and the other one Y. So the picture of a complete octave would look like this: Do, Re, Mi, X, Fa, Sol, La, Si, Y, and then the Do of the new octave. There are actually three enneagrams to each octave, not just one. Two borrowed octaves intersect the main octave in the following way:

In the readings of my series of writings, for instance, I will occasionally interrupt with something quite apart from the subject. Ordinarily these would be provided by the material itself. However, I decided to eliminate these artificial shocks contained in the writings themselves, and instead to prepare individuals to introduce these shocks and these missing notes during the readings that would be taking place, for future groups. When we toast the health of idiots, we wish for an individual that he find his true idiot, and we wish for him that he not crystallize his false idiot, and that it become subjective, but that he crystallize his true idiot, so that this can become for him objective material for work, not only data for his being, but also means by which the Absolute is able to manifest in his work.

The introduction of false idiots themselves constitutes a quite different octave. In order to do idiot work, one must understand the operation of the octave. Particularly one must understand that there are not one but three octaves that create objective octave. Man has only subjective octaves, octaves with seven notes.

O. could never understand this. He left my work. He began to become quite angry with me, because I introduced a peculiar octave to supply missing notes on the octave of his work. He wishes to be with me, and yet cannot be with me, because he does not understand this. Also because he cannot be humiliated. He does not understand the function of humiliation. He wishes to remain aristocrat. To be aristocrat in the Work means to maintain one's closed octave to the end of one's days.

S: The new "do" that happens in an octave. You said that is the first note of the new octave that is going to be.

G: It is a restorial for the previous octave, and introduces the next octave. It is two notes in one. This is why "do" is represented in objective music by a double note. Two notes are struck, which together make the higher octave "do." Because of harmonics, these notes can complete as the new "do," even though the note "do" itself has not been struck. The *chord* "do" has been struck.

For instance, there is a note 'C', but there is also a chord 'C major'. There is also a chord 'C minor', and 'C minor sixth', and 'C sixth', and 'C seventh', and 'C seventh diminished', and so forth. The chord C and the note C are exactly the same in function. The chord C can be created without the note C. The ordinary octave, with two notes missing, is the octave of involution. The octave with the two notes supplied by other octaves is the octave of evolution.

R: You said that the real octave has three components. There are two borrowed octaves connected to each octave?

G: We only see one note of each borrowed octave. If we see more than one note, we have fallen under its influence.

To avoid this requires will. To see the octave in its full progression requires attention. Attention and will are necessary for conscious octave.

J: Madame said earlier that the difference between impressions and perceptions is based on the knowledge of these two missing notes. You were relating it to action and ideas. Would this also be related to receiving perceptions or impressions?

G: If one uses the ordinary octave one receives impressions in only the false centers. If however one uses the real octave one receives impressions in real centers. One can also use genuine octaves to transfer impressions captured by false centers to real centers.

J: You are saying that we could transfer previously

received perceptions and make them impressions to the real
centers by later supplying the shocks?

G: Even finer material is still material. It must be carried
through some medium, from false centers to real centers. It
is no longer possible for you to receive these impressions, for
you are no longer young. But the impressions you received
when young, which all were absorbed by the false centers,
can be transferred to real centers, through the use of
intentional bridges. These must be real octaves and they
must encapsulate knowledge just like a space-ship and carry
it to the real center, where it can then be absorbed and stored
there as a substance for the real center. This is all in my first
series.

Madame: A basic element to complete that process is
attention.

G: Madame understands the function of attention perhaps
more than anyone else in my work. She can provide you with
all the data necessary for working with attention to collect
self and even for longevity. To begin with, small things, then
later big things can be done. If small things are not done
now, big things are not possible later.

C: Is the first step to take responsibility for oneself, or does
that come after one takes on the responsibility toward
others?

G: One cannot take responsibility for oneself so how can
one be responsible now for others? It is impossible to take
responsibility for oneself, in the beginning at least. Only
much later is one able to take responsibility for oneself. At
first one takes on responsibility greater than oneself. This
brings one outside oneself. Because in the beginning, one is
simply too many individuals to be able to take responsibility.

The sly man's way is to always work indirectly, always seemingly for something quite different. One begins work in another higher octave by taking suffering greater than one's own — but only slightly greater. Thus one is able to jump outside one's own skin. Then one is confronted suddenly with an objective obligation rather than with an obligation which is fragmented within oneself.

Madame: If we would take the responsibility for the teacher's work, then that is a tool to use for oneself. What I mean is, we cannot yet take the obligation toward suffering of the Absolute. That is something that we may do only in the position of a true individual. In order to get out of ourselves we could take some responsibility for the teacher's work. Is that useful?

G: Only if done correctly.

Madame: What are the correct elements of that?

G: For instance, my niece. She can take on obligation only because I discover conscience she has.

Madame: What are the correct elements of that?

G: Responsibility depends upon conscience. Obligation depends upon not only conscience but also knowledge. One becomes subject to a special law when one takes on obligation. When one takes on responsibility one is only subject to one's inner God. I allow someone only to take responsibility. I only require of them responsibility. Not for themselves tasks I give not directly, but through suggestion. If possible for them maybe I give obligation.

Madame: Obligation seems that it would need three elements to be working together; to *be able*, to *be*, and *to do*.

G: Of course. For instance, P. I can give task. Today he takes responsibility. On the other hand, Madame I can give not only responsibility, but obligation. Because I know she is able to speak for herself for entire period of obligation. She will not become subject, influenced, by her inner needs, by her inner personal suffering. Her personal suffering cannot stop her from fulfilling obligation. About P. I am not so sure. He has many personal sufferings. To him I only give small responsibility.

Madame: If we still have personal suffering we still have like and dislike as a product of personal suffering.

G: Even to the end of one's days one can have personal suffering. To have Will means that personal suffering does not interfere in obligation. We become subject to a greater law. M. has somewhat become subject to a greater law. He is able to be outside himself at least to the extent that he shares in my work a little. He is able to do work which I otherwise would have to fulfill. For instance, O. was not able to take on all of my work obligation. I asked him to do something impossible for him. Instead, he chooses something possible for him. He does not see that a new octave is necessary. When I hope the most on him to come back, other forces interfere. He becomes subject to another law, a law which is not beneficent.

This introduces maleficent law into my work. Many steps I have to take in order to eradicate. If he could come back before, he would not have made himself subject to these things. He becomes interested, he comes under the influence of social law, which has no being-value, which falls under influence of a greater law maleficent for the work, which governs outer life. When I gave him only responsibility, he was able to consciencely fulfill this. When I gave him obligation, his personal suffering interfered, he fell under its influence. He was forced to live subject to an octave introduced only for shock.

An afternoon talk

Madame: For me, when I have ideas I must express them; I can not be delayed or interrupted.

G: You must learn to hold an idea. For instance, suppose one sees the shock necessary in one octave, and yet the interval is not present at that time. One must learn to hold the shock and introduce it only then when it becomes necessary. If the shock is introduced too soon, it causes fragmentation of the octave.

J: Can we look at an octave in terms of geometry?

G: Geometrically the division is in unequal parts. We can see that there is a permanent tension between the notes do, fa, and sol. This permanent tension provides the inner force of the octave. Lines of tension represent transient forces within the octave. There are also temporary tensions; 1-4-2-8-5-7.

Temporary tensions borrow from the permanent tension in the octave. In order to do this there must be tensions introduced between "mi and fa" and between "si and do."

[57]

It must be understood then that the movement within the octave is not linearly from note to note, but through the influence of tensions. We see a tension existing between "mi" and "X," the missing note. At the same time, that tension also exists between "X" and "Y," the second missing note. In order to understand the function of the octave, one must see not only the octave which is visible to us but also the octave which is borrowed.

S: I understand the theory of the presentation, but there is a big gap for me in practical understanding. Would it be possible to make an example?

G: Theoretical is necessary before practical. Each Saturday evening I show practical function of octave in toasting ceremony. To understand this, however, one must know theory as well. Why I show idiot toasts? For my pleasure? Why do you think this was preserved? This is a practical means to demonstrate exact function of all laws operating, not only higher laws. Ordinary man always has desire to complete octave trying to arrive at his *idee fixe* of what completion of octave means. He urgently strives to reach "do" once again. He does not wish to be caught between two stools. In order to truly complete an octave, and then to bring that octave to the next higher octave, one must allow oneself the luxury of remaining in that octave longer than one would like, in order to make two more notes.

M: Earlier you spoke of three octaves which are needed to make an objective octave, and that these two other octaves are negative in nature. Their nature is negative.

G: No. They only represent negative force when introduced to another octave. Octave is convex until interval. Then at interval it becomes concave, and then convex once again. This represents negative influence which must be overcome.

S: I was just thinking that of all the notes of a borrowed octave only the one that is necessary is used.

G: If you do not understand how to use octaves then you can become influenced by them.

M: Is it correct to say that these two other octaves that have to be introduced are affirming and denying forces?

G: No. These are denying forces within the original octave. The first octave, the octave within which you work, is affirming. The other octaves provide denying force. Without such denying force no real movement is possible. Denying force can only be introduced consciously. Other octaves can be borrowed from anywhere. To borrow from another octave makes force of possibility. This force of possibility we call reconciling. Reconciling force is not original force, but *resulting* force.

M: Do, fa and sol are in constant tension?

G: Also in constant relaxation. They create because of constant tension, continual inner equilibrium.

M: Is it correct to say that you can assign the force of affirming, denying, and reconciling?

G: It is necessary to eradicate all subjectivity in perceiving the function of the octave.
   It is not sufficient to simply ask a question. One must ask a real question, as Madame pointed out earlier. To ask of someone to teach everything about baking bread is a question that cannot possibly be answered. Only if one has tried to bake bread, and is consistently doing wrong things, then this can be corrected. The sly way, the cunning way, is to understand not from below, even in theory, but instead to

increase greatly one's necessity and thus to be given for one's work in accordance with one's obligation and scale of suffering, higher bodies. Only when one has developed at least partially such higher bodies is it possible to understand in a real way. For instance one can know a great deal about the body of a giraffe, and yet it means nothing to one unless one has such a body.

You have undertaken the care and feeding of your planetary body, but until you undertake a greater obligation than your own given to you by nature, you have no reason to understand the laws which apply to a greater body than your own. If on the other hand, you take on obligations which make necessity, then it becomes necessary to know these laws. Everything you do, do in such a way that it exposes you to great danger, so that either the cosmos to which you are subject presently makes you *tchick* or you make it *tchick*. You become immortal within the limits of a lesser cosmos than that to which you are subject, because it is not a "restorial" for higher body substances.

M: What you said about not taking action — obligations will present themselves?

G: Nothing that you could learn how to do in an ordinary way will help you to take on obligations. Only special doing can make possible obligations. Otherwise, there is only wish to be obligated.

J: Then wish to be obligated cannot bring us to obligation?

G: No. But it can provide data for one's being. It also takes up a great deal of time. Time is very precious. You would not want this.

S: You talked about placing ourselves in real danger. I have some trouble appreciating what real danger is. Would real danger be something like if we were responsible for a group of people and did not get the information that was required for the next part in their work?

G: If I am obligated to give you everything necessary, as I have taken this obligation, I make special suffering for myself. Because of the necessities of my work, I have a certain time limit within which I must deliver to you all means necessary. Only after completion of such obligation is it possible for me to die and to take on entirely new obligation. My obligation can only take new form after old form is complete. For me, this completion is not simply to return, but to make completely new octave for my work. By law, nature must keep me alive. But law does not say I must give to everyone complete. I must transmit everything, but I can do this in such a way that it makes necessity for individuals to share with each other fragments which they have received.

J: You said earlier that your work with groups was just a very small part of your real work. So that means that even with the relationship to our group, to which you have given all necessary data in relationship to a part of your work, it is necessary to complete that. But even the completion or understanding of that part is not the understanding of your octave or your work.

G: In your present state you cannot possibly understand the scope of my work. You see everything linearly. A great deal of my work is not visible to you. I show you what I can. I hope for you with all my being, that you are able to see more as more obligation you take. So far I convince you to take very small obligation within octave of my work visible to you. Later you see more. When you see more, you understand greater necessity. You come out not only of yourself but also of your group. You become independently formed in work.

When you see possibility of greater scale, you understand laws of world creation and maintenance for all possible scales. You must study obligation. You see then that the whole secret rests with obligation.

R: It sounded to me as if responsibility is not directly pointed out. You give hints and if somebody responds to that responsibility then it gives you information about that person.

G: With what they respond?

R: It takes conscience to recognize that obligation exists.

G: Yes. Must have conscience at least partially formed in order to see possibility. For instance, when taking first small responsibility, someone must see beyond their own suffering, personal suffering, even beyond suffering of friends, even beyond suffering of the group, they must see my suffering.

J: Suppose someone sees part of your suffering for a short while.

G: Part of my suffering is useless to see. One must see, at least for a moment, everything about my work suffering. Even my personal suffering is now attached to work suffering, and falls under that law. Personal suffering only possible for non-entity. Without this, such individual ceases to exist.

M: How is seeing your suffering arrived at?

G: Through wish to help. First to feel my suffering. Then to wish to help. One is attracted to this special kind of suffering. A man for whom conscience is not formed a little, is not interested in suffering of other individuals. He can only see parts of it as they are provoked and aroused by the actions of life. He sees first the suffering of "re", and then the suffering of "mi", and then the suffering of "fa", then the suffering of "sol". He never sees their suffering *as a totality*. It is necessary to see the totality in order to see the absurdity of personal suffering.

M: It has to be objective.

G: One must feel pity for something greater than oneself. In order to wish to take some obligation of mine, you must pity my suffering. Only later can you pity higher suffering. Last one can pity oneself. When one is able to take responsibility for oneself. Now we arrive at the same "do" with which we began this talk, but on a different octave. To take advantage of this new octave, we must now move just a little past the first interval. If we stopped now we would return to the octave in which we began.

M: Is it necessary to take on an obligation to your work in order to see the suffering of your work?

G: No. Only necessary to pity greater than yourself, and to wish more suffering, not less. In ordinary life, everyone wish less suffering for themselves. They never voluntarily take greater suffering than their own. Only someone wishing to increase suffering to at least "three zeroes" am I interested in. But these three zeroes must be added to personal suffering, to make one thousand times present suffering provided by nature.

Even completed man can only take certain scale of obligation, and no further. To take more obligation one is no longer a human being. All movement through scales possible only through making necessity. Necessity only can be made by taking obligation corresponding to suffering of a greater scale.

J: To be able to get out of yourself you have to want something more for yourself, not just see that it is possible in theory.

M: You also have to see that it is possible.

G: No. You do not have to see that it is possible. For instance, I offer M. a piece of cheese just now. He does not wish to eat a piece of cheese because he does not wish to be bothered. He is now working on high ideas. Cheese to him represents an interruption. He does not understand how a piece of cheese can help him. I insist and I give him a piece of cheese anyway, because I know what function this fulfills in his personal octave. This is cunning. In order to make things happen one must know *how to do* in an entirely new way.

You come here because you wish to alleviate your own suffering. This I allow to attract you here. When you arrived, you began to work on your personal suffering. I wait until you see that this is impossible; that your own suffering cannot be alleviated by anything you do. Meanwhile, very cunningly, I introduce you a little at a time the idea that there is a greater suffering. Now that you hear this, you wish to get out of your personal suffering and into the greater suffering that you feel is somehow better than your own, and perhaps will not hurt as much. You must understand that you cannot escape your personal suffering; only take on greater suffering, *including* your own suffering. If true on a small scale, then also true on a greater scale. So if suffering even a little bit greater than your own exists, then you can see possibility of suffering much greater. If greater scales of being you are aware, then you have some idea on what scale this can occur. When you begin to feel greater suffering even one step removed from personal suffering, within your being you suffer accordingly. You begin thus to understand the suffering that I have taken upon myself; what this suffering must feel like for me. You must understand that I am small in the scale of things.

Also right now, if you feel suffering, you also feel corresponding pain. With greater suffering, corresponding pain diminishes and eventually vanishes. Pain is caused by interaction of suffering with identity. Only personal suffering produces pain. Greater suffering has in itself no pain.

J: What is the meaning, then, of suffering not in relationship to your identity?

G: Ordinary man does not always suffer. Sometimes he has pleasure. Sometimes he has alleviation of his suffering. But ordinary man believes in the *possibility* of perpetual pleasure. He does not understand that suffering is periodic no matter what he does to prevent it. Therefore all his life he devotes to seeking perpetual pleasure, and to avoidance of suffering, hoping that suffering will not visit him again. This is, of course, impossible. If you understand that even though you feel quite content just now, around the corner suffering is inevitable, then you wish to work. False hope eliminates inner necessity for work. You hear that the Absolute suffers. This means something to you.

S: Yes, it does.

G: You *feel* for the Absolute. This means you have beginning of conscience. Others come here only to extinguish their own personal suffering. They have no conscience for Absolute. But you feel as if you are created for some purpose.

S: All I know, really, is that there has been one steady signal all the way through, and it stopped the day that you spoke about the suffering of God. When I first arrived at the school it stopped a little bit, then wavered, then it started again when I got used to being here. Now there is a quiet inside that I have never experienced in life.

G: If you refuse obligation, then nagging begins again.

S: Yes. I know that.

G: You must feed this by paying back. Only then will it remain quiet.

J: It is hungry then?

G: You feed hunger of fulfilling obligation of Real Man. Most people never hear this incessant nagging, and therefore it does not bother them. This is why you are here in special group. All in this special group feel such remorse.

S: So we are drawn to where we can possibility begin to work towards the only thing that we feel as real. But then there is a big gap. There is a picture of a life going by and being drawn to something, having no idea what it really is. The purposes for life has led us to where we wished to go.

G: So Greater Octave is possible.

S: Yes. But the tools that we have are extremely limited. Whatever it takes to work is not available just yet.

G: I say already that life provides two rhythms. You live in water. Water is natural environment for you. How you can get on land and cross to other river, is for you now a big problem.

S: Yes. It is tormenting.

G: You must find way to take some water with you to

sustain you until you reach other river.

J: Is that the way then of feeding remorse?

G: No. Remorse only brings you here. It nags *everyone* until they come to school. But school only possible for some, not for everyone. This is why man suffers and why man who cannot come to this must be pitied. You on the other hand have some relief. There is one small thing inside which has now shut up. You cannot tell it to shut up. Only by coming to school will it shut up. This *reminding force* in you. Most people have learned to ignore, but you did not ignore. This makes you special. It makes you closer to candidate, even though not candidate exactly. But now you wish to make sure that this thing will by all possible means remain silent.

S: Maybe.

G: Now the nagging is quiet, you hear even worse voice.

M: The vacation is almost over.

G: The vacation has been over a long time ago. Until you do this thing, then it will continue to nag you even worse than the other. Sometimes people leave just to have ordinary nagging. Not even necessary for me to tell you what to do next. You do everything until you find thing that makes this inner demanding voice shut up. When you discover what it is that wishes to be done, that voice quiets. When *everything* is quiet inside, you become candidate for work. It takes a long time, maybe a very long time, before everything quiet inside. But now you have special inner meaning. When you pay debt to nature, everything quiet inside, you can hear whispering voice, which tells you how to do Work. Until then, too many voices too loud. You cannot hear whisper of small voice which tells you how to do Work.

Fragments of Ancient Knowledge

You look at the animal will as something alien to you. You cannot understand why you were identified with it; why you were even interested in it.

If you look back to childhood, you will discover that there was a time when you were not interested in anything that anybody else was interested in. You worked very hard to become interested in those things in order to belong and to achieve the status of a "member of the herd." You will discover that in order to form those interests, you were forced to develop a personality. If a shock had been applied at two points in your early life, you would never have developed those interests, nor would you have developed false centers. Children do not need to be taught anything in particular. They can be taught regular curriculum. If they are present at certain ages, a series of shocks can be applied. This was actively practiced anciently as a part of the ordinary process of a child's education. When this is introduced, then the diversion of impressions to false centers does not occur. The child can develop with essence intact, simply through the introduction of two major shocks in childhood. I hope to have a number of individuals of the school who are able to do that so that schools can be organized in which this can be introduced into the lives of children. Also, as I pointed out, this can be done with adults. The same two shocks can be introduced into an adult. However, in order to do that, first the transfer of psyche data has to take place to the essence only then can such shocks be introduced. An adult does not have time to get impressions proper to early childhood.

P: Does God suffer from the demands made upon him from the relative world? Which he from his own nature must respond to?

G: He made only one mistake, but a big one. He made umbrella when he should have given himself enema.

P: What happened as a result of this?

G: Now he wears galoshes and is an idiot just like the rest of us.

M: To see the suffering of God do we look to the world of form?

G: You wish that what I say is true. First that must die in you, then you are able to know impartially.

M: Is it a matter of seeing for ourselves the suffering of God, or being shown the suffering of God?

G: You do not have to see God in order to understand the suffering of God.

M: I did not mean seeing God. I meant, does one see the suffering of God or is one shown the suffering of God?

G: If you have greater being, then you are shown. Lesser the help you need, the more you are given.

   If you are concerned with the outcome, then you do not really belong in the Work. You must take the risk that it is all for nothing. I want you to understand that those individuals who crystallize as not useful to the work understood that they would not be useful to the work before they completed their crystallization. They also knew that there was a chance sometime in the future that they could become useful. If they had chosen the other way, then would they have accepted their ordinary destiny. As you begin to deeply view these questions, the more you will come to understand what I mean by study. Ordinary study is simply to hear these ideas and be able to repeat them at cocktail parties. Deep study is to focus all one's attention with the force of one's whole being, until it is completely understood.

A: I do not think I have ever experienced objective suffering. I do not really know what that is.

G: To deliberately suffer in this way is a form of self-pity. You do this to pretend you did not understand. Then when you have suffered sufficiently to justify righteous indignation you will leave, blaming me for results of your suffering. Everyone here is too much clever, not enough courage.

   If you knew the ancient method of prayer, then you could pay back for your arising. But first have to know the ancient use and the ancient method for prayer. It was lost during the closing days of the Babylonian civilization. They knew not only the use of prayer but how to pray. No longer is this known through ordinary means. It is not even contained in legominism. It was so commonly known, they never thought it necessary for legominism. Prayer as it is used today is useless in objective sense. All modern prayer is subjective. That is why I said that ancient religious ceremony was objective and that modern religious ceremony is entirely subjective.

J: Nothing is preserved of the objective in it?

G: There are some ancient pieces of knowledge that are preserved in the ritual of the churches, but *use* of ceremony is entirely subjective.
   Of what use is immortality all by itself? Why should our creator make the possibility for human beings? Man existed originally within the creation for the sole purpose of alleviating our creator's suffering.

A: You said that the Boddhisattva vow is not the same as the work.

G: Not at all the same. The Boddhisattva vow is compassion toward all other beings. The work is compassion toward the Absolute. Not all human beings are able to be willing to help God. It is a frightening idea to ordinary man that God might need help.

On conscience

Conscience can tell you how to act always and in everything in relation to the real world rather than morality which forces you to submit to all cosmic and planetary laws to which human beings are ordinarily subject.

The secret as I have already mentioned is to subject yourself only to one great law, the greatest law possible for yourself. I discovered quite by accident this means of perfecting oneself while trying in many different ways to attain for myself higher gradations of reason, higher emotions, and so on. When I say higher centers, I mean the development of essence centers as they should be.

Not counting those attainments unnecessary to completed man, I calculated the amount of time required to master each of these individually and collectively. The result of the said calculation was that to master just those things necessary for completion of man without quotation marks would require at least two hundred and fifty-six years, provided nothing went wrong.

I resolved first of all to elucidate experimentally what it was that the complete puzzle made when put all together, in order to understand just what use each of these attainments would be to a perfected man.

I came to understand eventually that even with mastery of all manifestations proper to perfected man they would not in themselves make possible the full attainment of completed man. On the other hand these attributes do not need to be mastered at all by a completed man. A real man is able to be and to do with no effort to master the said attributes. Along with this came the realization that only in a complete form are these attributes of any genuine value.

After a while I discovered the means by which one can cunningly direct oneself in a path around the aim of completed man in such a way that perfection can be achieved indirectly. Only later did I come to understand that indirect means are the only means possible.

The secret which I have already mentioned to you is to choose a law and become subject to it, at the same time becoming as valuable as possible to it. There is, of course, a small fee involved…a minor thing, of no concern. It is that you permanently and forever give up for yourself your chance for union with God. After obligation there will be for you no place to rest, but for the first time you will have a real purpose in life, even though not your own, and the aim of which is beyond your imagination.

The cosmic pumping station

Man as we find him in nature is a pump, pushing finer matter into the outer world as it descends from the Central Sun-Absolute. His ordinary function is to solidify the outer world.

The secret of crossing from one river of life to the other is to reverse this pump, to draw gross matter back inside, transform it into its original form of independent arising as fine matter, and then to direct it back toward its place of origin, the Sun-Absolute. To do this is called Objective Prayer.

Ordinary man does not know how to do this, although he was able to do this a long time ago. He has long since refused this obligation because he prefers to receive energy and use it for his own purposes.

Ordinary man eats food and makes shit. Real Man can eat shit and make food. He sends food first to the astral body. To make food for the astral body he must transform specific substances, the result "si 12," in the food octave.

At least some part of the effort to prepare for work is to discover how to do. I only give "cathode beginning" of understanding.

In order to arrive at understanding of knowledge it is necessary to immerse yourself completely, arousing without remorse the all-centers-disappointment resulting from not being told everything step by step at all costs by Saturday afternoon. This has the desirable effect of making in your inner world the approximate action — only interiorly, of course — of a charnel house in full operation. Even though everything on the inside is in a complete uproar, however, everything outside must remain completely passive.

By trying to do with these ideas you are able to learn. Only questions may be raised. This interior uproar is partly a method, but the turmoil must be about an important question. Inner turmoil is for ordinary man always over some trifle or other in his outer life.

Ordinary inner turmoil continually changes its center of gravity, depending on influences external and internal. Intentional "yes-ing and no-ing" always has the same center of gravity.

Several questions can be active within one's inner world all proceeding at once to make turmoil, but center of gravity of all serious questions is always *exactly the same place*. (He emphasized this very strongly.) In the same way, *real "I"* never changes its center of gravity.

If you use only those muscles necessary to accomplish an outer activity the body can be eventually made passive. If only those emotions necessary are activated according to the requirements of the moment, the whole of outer life can be "passified."

All centers as they are now are used to feed the outer world; what is called in objective science *the moon*. This pump is going entirely as nature intended, directing everything from inside toward the outside. Ordinarily, then, man is a cosmic apparatus for taking food from the inside and pushing shit to the outside.

To reverse the pump it is necessary to first learn to "passify the outside", and then to learn to take from air and impressions those substances necessary for the transformation of shit into higher food not for the moon. In order to understand this idea it is necessary to know that everything is material, even thought.

For ordinary man, what would be his astral body is his denying force, because he allows his physical body to be the active part of himself. In this effort we must strive to be outerly passive and innerly active. Eventually the whole outer world becomes passive, and denying force is the pushing force needed to send finer substances upward.

Afterwards the connecting force between these two bodies occurs so that they can be treated as one denying force for the causal body. The method for doing this is preserved in legominism in the following way: Make the inner as the outer and the outer as the inner, then make the two one.

Ordinarily one feeds the body, mind and emotions with impressions. Because the results of these foods do not pass beyond the first octave, one feeds the moon when one feeds oneself. To reverse this trogoautoegokratic process the inner world must receive impressions completed above the tritacosmic octave. One feeds in this way the inner world with the *results of results* of the outer world.

To elucidate this for yourself you must tear out all your hair until you have a shiny pate as I do. Only then after such voluntary suffering will you have the Will necessary to reverse the pump.

Through struggle with yourself can you become able to do this. Not, however, through ordinary struggle.

For the body to become passive does not mean that it must cease all activity. To make the planetary self passive one must lose interest in the outer world without also losing interest in what is occuring.

Madame mentioned that she had been a dancer for many years, although she is no longer practicing as a professional artist. In the beginning she did this because she felt that it offered some future promise for her egoistic aims. Now, however, she does this just to keep her body in harmony. When she first came here, force of habit caused her flow of associations to compose innerly those dance movements she would do if on stage when music played. Now she is able to visualize or not visualize herself dancing as she chooses. When one is able to choose in this way, one has passified the outer world.

The secret to this is to find your genuine center of gravity. When we are able to keep the center of gravity inside, the outer world becomes automatically passive.

For instance, E. has a child. This child represents to her everything she hopes for. If the child remains for her a center of gravity in the outer world then her child becomes for her the active force. Then all her energy is directed from inside to outside. In this way she makes for her child also an active force, preventing formation of real will and ability to do in the child.

If on the other hand she does everything with her child just for her own inner world with her center of gravity remaining inside, her child can become for her the passive force, pushing special substances upward. She can use her child in this way and at the same time be of service to her child in the formation of everything proper to man preparatory to responsible age.

Only if her child provides this function for her inner world can she love him. If the child remains her outside center of gravity she can never really love her child because inwardly at least she knows that her child is costing her more than just her life. Even though a mother wishes to give her life for her child, this is not the means for providing what the child will need for responsible age.

Ordinary impulse of motherhood is to make the child one's

outer center of gravity. In order to genuinely love a child one must learn to take from the child what is one's own. The child is then forced to make his own inner world his center of gravity, thus preparing him for life in the real world.

Formation of real centers

If your centers had formed in essence we would not now be facing a difficult task before even the smallest preparation for Work is possible. We must transfer all impressions from personality, where they have been diverted since childhood, to the essence, thus making possible the formation of real centers of gravity. It is only these real centers which can be connected with each other.

Even after we accomplish this one cannot expect to be as a result more than fifteen years in essence age, but such as it is this is a big thing.

The demands of mechanical civilization inevitably claim a child by the age of five unless some extraordinary shock occurs to prevent crystallization of the personality. I have myself delivered such shocks to certain children in order to prepare them for my work in the future. Eventually they will appear and take my place in the Work.

Something similar to personality must form in order for an

individual to be able to function in contemporary civilization, but it does not necessarily have to form as the personality. The same impressions which make personality are those useful to the essence and which, if not diverted to false centers of gravity, provide just that material necessary to develop the essence as a three centered being.

At the age of five there comes what can be called a divergence. This occurs at an exact tangent to the natural development of essence centers. Then again another divergence occurs at the development of the intellectual center. This is at the mi-fa interval. Unless an outside shock is introduced false centers will automatically develop. The real thinking center cannot possibly develop if the false emotional center has already crystallized. Everything depends upon everything else in the machine. The divergence of impressions from essence to personality causes the almost complete collapse of initiative. In order to regain even ordinary will common to real man, this initiative must be rehabilitated through transfer from false to real centers of all impressions taken since the first divergence in childhood.

You cannot develop yourself. All attainments occur automatically only in accordance with the momentary necessity of the Work, and only in connection with one's individual obligation within the Work.

There is nothing you can do to change being directly. A real change in being is only possible to an individual who has been accepted into the Work. Such attainments are completely natural to one who has accepted a mission which requires higher being than ordinary man.

Faith, love and hope develop automatically as a result of one's continued efforts in the Work. There is no other way to do this.

Terror of the situation is a response *apropos* to obligation on a big scale. It at least shows that you are able to taste, if you cannot see.

You came here for your own reasons. What may confuse

you is that there are hundreds of schools which offer mastery of certain powers. What you may not realize is that taken as a whole these are all simply different aspects of a completed man. They belong to him, and even though it is possible to master several of these attainments individually, just mastery of aspects do not confer a change in being nor do they lead to completion.

For instance, if you were a horse, it would be natural for you to have a mane, fetlock, and so forth. In the same way all those things which are presently individually interesting to you are given automatically as tools for accomplishing your Work. Unfortunately for your egoistic aims, however, you cannot apply these powers outside the Work. They can only be applied as the needs of the Work dictate.

This means that in some cases even though you may have an impersonal reason to activate work powers, for instance to cure someone of cancer, you cannot do it. This provides unconscious suffering which can be useful for one's aims.

The influence of the Work is such that once in it you cannot divert yourself even a little from its path. One is subject to only one law, but one is subject to that law absolutely. One becomes more and more law-conformable as the scale of laws to which one is subject becomes higher and higher.

I should mention, by the way, that your chief weakness will not only not be eliminated, but will be crystallized as an idiot permanently, thereby dashing all your hopes for purification. You would not wish this for yourself with vanity and self-love, because you do not wish to be objective idiot in any respect. But I assure you that a chief weakness is necessary as channel for higher influences in order to direct you in the Work. This is a wish contrary to your nature, perhaps even to your present whole being. As you are now, you would not like it.

Law of work

The law of the Work is "conscious-participation-in-reciprocal-maintenance-toward-the-Sun-Absolute". Work comes before completion. Of course you are only given that gradation of reason necessary for you to do Work. Therefore if you wish for youself a higher degree of reason you must somehow increase necessity.

If you were a janitor and were given the task to clean a floor you would need a broom. If you wished to clean it more deeply a scouring brush and mop would be required. The same is true of Work. One is given only that which is necessary in order to accomplish sacred task. In that case attainments appear and disappear not in accordance with personal egoistic wishes but according to the needs of the Work at that time.

You must understand that when I say "law" I do not mean results. Real laws are beings who by interaction create certain definitized manifestations which we are able to see. One can align oneself with one such law and by doing so one can work for a being who directs a part of the Work.

Each of these sacred cosmic individuals is responsible for one aspect of the Work in the form of obligation to help God the Absolute.

In order to accept obligation to Work, one must study these beings and learn how to become useful to one of them. For instance, one such sacred individual has become crystallized in the highest possible body below the Absolute in the form compassion. Another has become representative of the highest possible form of Justice. All such higher beings exist, at least for the duration of the Work, in the relative and cannot merge with the Absolute. They direct the Work from Theomertmalogos, using beings who have attained individuality combined with ability to wish and to do.

In preparing for Work, one studies several objective sciences, among which are the science-of-obligation, science-of-service and science-of-sacrifice.

Science of sacrifice is also known as science-of-impersonal-suffering. These cannot be studied just willy-nilly. As one ponders more deeply the essence nature of each common cosmic sacred individuality one becomes as much as possible part of that individual by absorbing into oneself as great a part of the suffering of that individual as one is able.

Those sent from above come to remind men that they have forgotten their obligation to the Absolute. One learns all about the history of messengers sent from above in the objective science-of-obligation.

There are only so many great laws and only so much obligation available. As I have mentioned before, everything is material, even obligation and knowledge. When one becomes subject to one of these sacred individualities, one is no longer subject to any other law, including all other beings representing the Work on the level of cosmic maintenance. Other laws operate which are not beneficent; which are directly opposed to the Work.

These other laws not conforming to the Work are responsible for the introduction into the life of man just those ideas which serve to puff up their egoism, vanity and self-love. For instance, as a result of these other, maleficent laws, most of contemporary society believes that Mr. God will give them every little thing they desire, if only they pray very hard for themselves. And if they do not receive everything they want, they become angry with Mr. God and call Him everything under the sun. According to these same ideas, they also believe that their Mr. God is very sorry everyone is suffering and He wishes only to make this planet of ours into a "hunky-dory" place just covered with nothing but amusement parks and casinos; in short, a place where everyone can enjoy life to the fullest without having to pay a penny.

Motives of the teacher

Every moment that I spend with you is very precious. I have a lot of time, but only so much work time, and of this work time I have very little to spend with groups. In connection with this idea, I would like your impression of what I did last night.

R: Making us see that we were here for the wrong reasons.

G: No, I was not interested in that at all. I am doing work with you only in connection with my own obligations and suffering. I am trying to pull you into my suffering just a little, not all at once and by no means to the scale on which I have obligated myself to the Work, but at least when you help me a little in my work you begin to see your personal suffering in perspective; what a nothing it is compared to the scale of possibility for a man.

C: Last night you completely turned around what we thought were our intentions.

G: Why would I wish to do this?

[88]

M: To get us to examine why we are here, perhaps.

G: This is not true.

D: Then it was to get us to choose which path we want to follow.

G: No. You have not hit the mark.

D: To provide the experiences missing in us since childhood.

G: All this proves that you did not listen to what I said before. You do not connect one moment of experience with another. You remain fragmented while trying to understand.

S: Was it to wake us up a bit?

R: You have the responsibility to warn people who come to work with you?

G: No, you come here on your own responsibility. That is not it at all.

V: To make certain the group does not crystallize in the wrong way?

G: I do not care if the group crystallizes or not, except objectively with pity. I do not care for you at all subjectively until you become, for my efforts, a worthwhile candidate for work. Just now I am looking you over. You answer my question as if everything I do I do for you, as if you were my center of gravity. I cannot afford to care what happens to you, although in a small way I do care. I cannot afford to arrange my work and life obligation around you. When spare time is provided in my own work then I have time for you, but I do not look for spare time from work with you for my own work. It is the other way around from the way you see it.

Last night what I did had to do with the presence here of one of X's chief pupils. Do you not understand that everything I said last night will almost certainly be reported verbatim to X, who will in a few days spout it out exactly as if he had only just thought of it himself? He has become for many people an imaginary source for my ideas. It does not matter who said it first or best. He has public exposure. He likes my ideas, and likes to repeat them as his own. This is to my interest, although egoistically I would prefer otherwise. I did not mind having you watch me work last night, but it was not for you in particular. All I offered last night was hospitality. It would be better for you if you understand that not everything I do is for your sake, but for the sake of my own work, in which you play a very small part. Egoism makes you wish to be a spiritual big-shot, but you do not want to pay the price.

On slavery

Work is accomplished in very small things, much as a slave or janitor would do. In order to become a slave you cannot be too proud. You certainly do not need a great deal of knowledge to be a slave. What kind of knowledge does a slave need? You have no real use for many things you think you would like to have for yourself.

It is even too much for you now to ask you to close a door each time you enter, or to pull plug when you use the water closet. If you cannot even consider these things, how then can you hope to work to alleviate the suffering of the Absolute?

Even if you do everything just exactly right, there is still no guarantee that you will be accepted as a slave. To be objective slave is a big thing. You can wish to be such a slave, and yet for one reason or another not become being a slave. For example, maybe you do not have a big weakness. If you do not have a very big weakness you are no good as objective slave.

R: I cannot know yet if what you said before about the Work being to relieve the suffering of God is true or not.

[91]

G: This is too bad, I cannot help you determine truth, just as you cannot build Taj Mahal by sitting on ass. I am not the one to ask; maybe my answers are true, maybe not. I only suggest questions to you, which you may decide are for you gravity center questions which must be at all costs answered. To answer them, you cannot simply turn them back to me. I could tell anything and you might believe me. But of course you are lazy, and are willing to pay the price of laziness, which is suggestibility.

J: You mentioned efforts of a different kind. How might we go about making such efforts if we don't know what they are?

G: I could tell how I do, but this will not do good for you.

J: I am still unable to grasp any of this.

G: I hope you do not try, but if you insist to grasp, you get no more than if on a carousel. To hold in your hand these ideas is to take to yourself much mechanical suffering.

V: You said yesterday that it would be dangerous for us to remain here with you. Why is this?

G: Better for your safety to be in a tradition. I am wild horse. What if I am not objective, perhaps only saying things to make you feel attracted to my work? Maybe I am on the side of the fallen angels, and you are asked to join unhappy band of sinners. I might reject union with God for other reasons than those I tell....Perhaps I said this only to arouse in you pity for me. Along with this, maybe everything I ever say to you is nonsense. If so, you can lose everything, all chances for your being, to remain with me. More so, I know that when telling you this you feel more attracted just because I tell you to go away. I by law must tell these ideas so you are forced to ponder them. You are still young, not yet crystallized into my work. You still have a chance to do something else for your being. I am little; not big enough to take responsibility for you. If you stay here you are responsible for whatever happens to you. In traditions, they responsibility for you take.

S: How can I work on myself right now? Is there anything I can do to make it easier for me to come here each day and work with you?

G: You come here with complete garbage questions, mostly concerned with your own personal suffering, which is as far as you are concerned, quite unique in the cosmos. You cannot even begin to ask real questions until you become of responsible age, which means to take more suffering than presently you have. Before this, of course, it is necessary for you to see a suffering greater than your own. Just now, you cannot imagine such a thing.

D: How can we learn to see greater suffering?

G: I do not know. I cannot even give you shovel with which to dig. When you take a question it is your responsibility to answer it. To find answer, you may have to dig very deep. No one can tell you how or where to dig; you must find for yourself. I have told you questions for myself which forced me to dig deep, but I do not tell you how for you. I cannot make change for your being, I can only create conditions for change.

T: Do you have to develop at least a few things before taking obligation?

G: If there were a stable and much shit in, nobody would expect you to work without shovel and broom. In work, when you need shovel and broom, you get shovel and broom.

When you no longer need them, they are taken away from you. A slave owns nothing; is given tools for work to do as he is commanded. Work that offers only the shovel and broom is shit itself. Attainments are simply the means for fulfilling obligation.

B: I stay here even though I am afraid. I think I remain mostly because it is more difficult here than anywhere else.

G: You only imagine difficult. You like to get yourself into horrible situations so you can feel fear. It is the only emotion possible for you without extra effort, so you like it. You think that by difficulty it makes you a slave any faster?

J: What steps can one take to admit one's weakness?

G: To admit? Of weakness you should be happy, proud, even. It makes possible work on yourself and obligation someday. If you cannot see chief fault then you have not self-observed.

J: Admitting a fault would be working with it?

G: You cannot work with it, only make from it an idiot, either subjective or objective. That is the possible kernel of your being. To make pearl it is necessary to have grain of sand, then pearl can be coated around it. Pearl "Karatas" cannot form itself around a nonentity.

M: How can we decide which law to align ourselves to?

G: First of all you must study all laws, not only of maintenance, but also of creation. Of destruction you do not need to know anything. When you understand more, by that time you will also be able to do more. Then perhaps you can decide intelligently not only which law you are attracted to, but also which law you are best able to work for.

M: Crystallizing the enlightened idiot and the ordinary idiot as objective, do they both serve the same function?

G: For you this is a very good question. Ordinary idiot can still be helped by God. Enlightened idiot even God cannot help; because he has no conscience. He can only acquire such by consciencely descending to ordinary idiot.

M: How can an ordinary idiot acquire conscience?

G: By becoming enlightened idiot.

S: Is it important to develop conscience?

G: No. Only important if one wishes to be in the Work. For ordinary life it is not only unnecessary, it is embarrassment.

B: How then can we use you?

G: I do not know. I have heard some ideas proposed by your group, and to my opinion they are all quite madcap.

A wee bit more about slavery

We were talking today about those who could not surrender to the Work. When they were told they must think like a slave, obey like a slave, surrender like a slave, but not work like a slave, they did not understand, and so they were forced by inner considering and *idee fixe* to leave the Work.

A man must be a slave only to God, and even then he must remain internally free. Lords and ladies try to cling to their aristocracy and yet become a slave. Self-love, vanity and false pride are not becoming to a slave. To be a genuine slave one must not only say "yes," but "yassuh!" with all one's being. Real pride is to be a slave in the Work. This is the only kind of pride which will not cause downfall.

You can be a slave to your own personal suffering, a slave to your inner evil God. I do not ask that you go all the way to the top of the ladder. I know this is not possible for you now. Only later does this become real factor. Right now you are *merde de la merde,* shit of shit. But angels are silly creatures. They were never shit...And so, when one man arrives perfected in heaven there is more rejoicing than if one hundred angels reached the same gradation of reason, just because he came from shit.

I only ask you to take one step, such as you are. This small step would be to take for yourself some of my obligation, to join Work suffering. I can allow you to do this knowing that I will be forced to accept a new, unknown form of suffering in exchange. The amount of suffering for which I am obligated never changes except to increase. In this way it is possible without knowledge for you to come a little way out of your personal suffering.

Ordinary man does not understand this "little trick", for they wish to make their suffering less than minimum obligation for man. To try to escape this small suffering of theirs makes their ordinary suffering even worse.

One cannot reduce the minimum obligation to nature for a human being to less than nothing. How could it be less than this? For a three-brained being to take the obligation of a one- or two-brained being is a sin, but man as he is commits this sin every day. He should feel organic shame, but as he is he feels nothing whatever except a vague urge to become just a bit more comfortable.

It is the way of the sly man to take larger obligation and suffering. Of course you cannot see right now how to do this for yourself. But it is possible for you to take some of my obligation as apprentice sufferer. You think that to take on more suffering is to take to yourself more pain. But pain exists in you only because your being has outgrown your present obligation. Pain tells you to become more than you are, to step outside yourself just a wee bit more.

The greater the obligation, the more voluntary the suffering.

Sponsorship

If one wishes to be admitted to an exclusive club, one must have a sponsor who is already in the club, and along with this you must be qualified for membership. In the case of a social club it is a question of family and money. In the case of the inner circle of mankind, it is quite a different question altogether. For that club one must also have a friend already in the club, but neither family nor money will open the door for you.

The idea of sponsorship is very important. It is on the same scale as the idea of voluntary suffering and creation of an external devil for continual wakefulness. It is not as important as the idea of obligation, but even obligation is not possible without a sponsor.

The planetary body is a sponsor for being on earth. This idea can be applied on every scale. If a law is true, it is always true, only the scale is different.

For the inner circle of humanity you must have a sponsor who is already a member in order to be accepted. You must be able, and also housebroken. No one would sponsor someone who always breaks the china whenever things do not go exactly right. For example, if I sponsored P. for the inner circle, I would have to feel able to guarantee his manifestations and his ableness. If they ask me about him, I must be willing to say that he did not break the china in my house, and that he was able to help me in my work. If I sponsored him and he misbehaved or was not strong enough to take the ableness, the consequences for my work would be very bad on a very large scale.

In this club the members always have a special relationship. No matter how they feel about each other's manifestations they are obligated to treat each other always with respect. Mood has no place in real work.

R: Is there ever a time when we could sponsor ourselves?

G: Only he who can kiss his own lips while standing on his own shoulders can sponsor himself in this club of a different kind.

Group effort

Group effort does not alleviate the suffering of God. Alleviation of suffering of the Absolute can only be accomplished by beings who have become real individuals working consciously and taking obligation intentionally. Groups are only for the preparation of such individuals.

A being who is in the Work must sometimes take responsibility to develop such groups in order to partially prepare others. A group is not intended to continue endlessly. Once a few individuals are found who are possible candidates for preparation, everyone else is sent away and the group dissolved.

You are not here to learn anything or to attain for yourself a few powers, but to prepare for Work. I can only offer preparation for candidacy and cannot tell in advance whether this preparation will be productive or not. Nothing is guaranteed. For me to risk precious time you must show your resourcefulness and the result must be commensurate with my effort toward you.

Do not misunderstand the group work. It is simply the basis for bringing together all possible candidates for initiation in one place so that I can measure potential of each one in relation to the others, then decide toward which ones my efforts would be most directly placed.

Vows

C. is probably the most powerful example of someone who is motivated entirely toward his own self-interest. He has almost no consideration for anyone around him. This is his chief weakness. Perhaps you think I say this just to shame him publicly, but in reality I can give him much more to work with than most of you, because your fear of humiliation is too great for you to have shown your big weakness just yet.

D. barely hears anything outside himself. Because of this isolation of his, he believes himself to be completely unique. In his case isolation protects his vanity.

I cannot break in from the outside. I do not wish to. In order to break down those barriers they would have to assume even more suffering than is natural to them, on a much larger scale than they wish to have now. If this does not break the shell, it at least makes it transparent so that they are able to see that there is something or other outside them, even if they are not certain what it is.

This is a great secret of the Work; by simply extending suffering onto a larger scale, one can increase at the same time completely automatically one's perception, range of impressions and ability to hold and split the attention.

To try to increase these directly is like hay trying to enter an elephant from the wrong end.

L: Is taking responsibility part of obligation?

G: Obligation and responsibility are two totally different ideas. You may have responsibility to your family and to your boss, but obligation can only be to the Work. While responsibility depends upon the impulse of duty, which can change from day to day its focus of attention, obligation never alters its center of gravity, and depends for its actualization entirely upon conscience.

Today you may feel responsible toward something or other, and tomorrow you do not. But if today you take obligation, tomorrow you cannot wriggle out of it.

P: Would you say then that you are receptive to obligation and active toward responsibility?

G: In the west this whole question is misunderstood because there is no objective morality nor is there subjective learning to replace it, as there is in civilizations which have resulted from ancient knowledge and maintained knowledge of how to live through tradition if not through conscious data. For example, T. built a big monastery in America not understanding that Americans are notorious for deciding this year that monastic life is very fashionable, and next year that it is *passe*.

Today T. is forced to sell his monastery and live in near-poverty, just in the same way that I was forced to sell everything when I discovered this maleficent defect in western life. Americans and English do not keep their vows; they do not take them seriously at all. They do not take vows of obligation, they take vows of whim. It would be unthinkable in the east for someone to behave so unbecomingly, but here and in America they take vows the way they take aspirin.

"Philadelphia"

R: In your talks to the American groups, you said that self-observation is a particular focus for American groups, whereas self-remembering is a particular focus point for English groups. This made me think that possibly they are more similar than one might at first imagine.

G: Wrong you are. Self-remembering is emotional. Self-observation mental. Emotional appeals more to English. Intellectual appeals more to Americans. Everyone wants what they do not have. This forces those who think to feel, and forces those who rely on feelings to think a little.

R: Do they both serve the same purpose equally well?

G: Eventually, no matter what one starts with, one must go to Philadelphia. After Philadelphia all roads are the same.

R: Does that mean something?

G: Why you ask?

R: It makes me snicker, I think it is cute. I wonder how much I see cuteness when you really are trying to say something.

G: Everyone must go to Philadelphia. Everyone thinks I mean American Philadelphia. But...To understand this, they must discover true meaning of 'Philadelphia'. Everyone must go to "City of Brotherly Love", then all roads are the same.

To be consistent

In order to be able to tense certain muscles in body and relax other muscles in body you should divide your body and attention into different portions. Tighten the left hand only while everything else is relaxed. Tighten the left jaw, the right buttock and the abdomen while everything else is relaxed. Whenever a word is uttered, either by yourself or by someone else in your presence, speed up internal tempo and note the reverberation of each word sounded in your common presence. Learn to generate new postures. Refine your daily life so that you are consistent in everything. Only then is real change possible. To know what should be changed, you must be the same from day to day, even if to be the same in this way is very bad in your self-estimation. You change from day to day, jumping from posture to posture, because you are embarrassed at your present postures. This is why self-study is impossible for ordinary man. His vanity is too great. He does not wish to see himself, and when he does see himself he wishes to change from present postures to other more unaware postures. You of course should not force this to stop, but you should observe when postures change in yourself and in others. As long as you are inconsistent, there is no way to correct the machine. It is operating erratically.

IV

The physical body of man; its possibilities and manifestations according to law

In order to assure myself, according to my, by now long established aim that all the data necessary for the formation in your common presences of a complete understanding of the possible manifestations of the physical body of man and the laws to which these manifestations are subject, it is first necessary, before I begin, to clarify for you certain principles now operating within the sphere of human life on Earth.

It is in the first year of life that humans gain nearly all of the manifestations available to them for the whole of their lives. Only a few changes in possible manifestation can be introduced after that time. It is in the first five years of life that the specific crystallizations of these manifestations are determined; so that after the fifth year of life not even a change in the outward appearance of the manifestation is to be expected. These possible manifestations or as we will call them, postures, are learned in the moving, emotional, and intellectual centers and in the essence itself.

When we say that a man is not a Man until he has all possible manifestations of a man, we mean that he may not have completed a particular center in the early formatory period, that is in terms of all possible manifestations of that particular center. He may have chosen only three or four manifestations as necessary to him. Even if he somehow should form the wish in himself, however contrary to nature, to do something quite different from his ordinary manifestations, this can occur ordinarily only as a result of mixing two or more of these original manifestations to which he has limited himself. Later in life if he comes to study hatha yoga, he will be able to form postures only in relation to these same three or four possible physical manifestations. If he studies dance, he will have the same limitations. Even though he may appear to have many more manifestations, he will only actually have combinations of these. This is why a great many dancers and actors are in an objective sense bad performers. An actor must have not only many physical manifestations but also emotional postures. If he only has three or four possible emotional postures in his repertoire, he must imitate, limited by his ordinary manifestations. The manifestations of additional emotional postures are impossible for him. In ancient acting, real actors could assume any emotional posture, or intellectual posture required to play a role.

Madame: Is an example of that Shakespeare?

G: Shakespeare did not write for real actors. He wrote for actors who could not act. This is why he was forced to write in the *bon-ton* literary style of his day. Because an actor could represent only his own emotional type, he had to explain his feelings verbally rather than emanate it as in ancient performances. During ancient times, a man would get exposed in the first year of his life to all possible manifestations. Children were shown how to accept each of these manifestations no matter how displeasing. The people who taught these things through "sacred acting" knew how each of these would be of use in adult life. In those days a harmonious education meant to teach all possible manifestations of all three centers, and also, through other means, to demonstrate all possible manifestations of essence.

Children feel free to imitate others without shame. Because of this they are able to manifest many more postures than adults restricted to their own type. So for instance they may learn how to manifest like F. whose manifestations we particularly think from one standpoint are not at all to be admired or imitated and yet a child must have complete access to all possible manifestations, even those that seem to be bad. B. does not like N.'s manifestations at all. The children do not know good from bad. They do not feel this way about it. They will imitate N., B., M., or K., or anybody else; they are all equally interesting to them just now. They do not discriminate between one and another manifestation. All manifestations to them are equally useful in their play. Perhaps later they will discard many of these due to expressions of displeasure from those adults and playmates they admire.

In the highly abnormal contemporary life, children are exposed to only a very few manifestations. They would never receive impressions of manifestations from every possible type.

In ancient times all families were large; it was more tribal. Children were subjected to all members of the community. Everyone in the community was responsible to all children; all children were required to come into contact with all members of the community, young and old. And because of this, they formed in themselves certain predictable impressions covering the whole range of human life. This is why a community of work is necessary for children even more than for adults. But adults can learn also under special conditions, although their early learning capacity has long since been lost. They first can learn to expand their possible manifestations of movement, then increase the number of possible manifestations for them in thought, then finally, in emotions. Since in man as nature makes him the centers do not operate simultaneously, the necessary impressions must arrive at precisely the right moment in the appropriate center. Of course with real knowledge, it is possible to predict when a certain center will become active.

Among everyone here at present, manifestations of all types are represented. If not for that, I would be forced to provide them. This situation has to be established artificially because contemporary society is unable to provide such function. Parents today tend to allow only those people to come to their homes and to play with their children, whose manifestations they prefer — which means manifestations conforming only to their own, and which have more or less the same limits. People do not generally allow visitors in their homes whose manifestations upset them. This means that many possible manifestations are never seen by children. Even in school, there is conformity of manifestation, and in any case by the time children reach school age, it is already too late. The possible interactions of children in schools is very limited.

The general manifestations of each child's school are different from the manifestations allowed in another child's school. Types never mix fully in those cases. Perhaps twenty-five manifestations are possible for a totality of impressions. Impressions are the most valuable substance for the formation of being. Our society today is composed of isolated pockets of culture, where every type seeks out its own type. Type depends wholly upon choice of manifestations. For instance, if an individual chooses three manifestations in the moving center, four in the emotional, three in the intellectual, and two in the essence, and only those, we say that he is one type, whereas if he chooses totally different, quite different manifestations, we would say that he is another type. If he chooses only one manifestation out of a possible three manifestations for that type, he would still be categorized as that type, even though two manifestations are missing.

In order to then learn the science of idiots, one must learn the specific categories of each type, and which manifestations fall into each category. Then one can properly and scientifically divide people into types. When one knows the type of an individual, then one can know all his possible manifestations. The aim in this respect is to increase one's manifestations so that one grows out of one's natural type, formed accidentally in childhood, and form a work type, composed of all manifestations possible for man not in quotation marks.

The astral body of man; its possibilities and manifestations according to law

We talked earlier about the body kesdjan. When we speak of completing the astral body we must think in terms of using new substances, although the substances are made of the same things as ordinary substances, crystallized in much the same way, but on a different scale. The primary substances used in filling the body kesdjan come from the "si 12" of the food octave, aided by the air octave. The air octave is a higher octave which brings lower substances of first food through the interval. Without this higher energy to pull it up, it cannot go past that interval. The method for doing this is to combine higher with lower substances, and the results rise through the interval as if higher substances. Air is second food of a higher octave. By mixing air with ordinary food, we bring first food substances into a higher octave. The way this happens is this: the food first enters the body at *do*. Then it goes through *re* and *mi*. It cannot ordinarily proceed past this

[114]

point unless it is helped from outside. In order for help to intervene, another octave is introduced. In order to fully process food, to make it a substance for our higher being body, three different octaves must come into play. The main octave is the octave of food. To this octave we introduce the octave of air. At the next interval, we introduce the octave of impressions. These three octaves are thus interconnected. The *do* of the air octave is introduced and provides a new note between *mi* and *fa*, a note which we will call *X*. The *do* of the impression octave, provides the note which we shall call *Y*, between *si* and *do*.

Everything man chews and swallows he calls food automatically. This is not food at all. From these substances first being food is extracted through the use of saliva, hydrochloric acid, and so on. First food is prepared through mixing of ordinary food with the assisting substance, saliva. Then it goes into the stomach, and it is prepared further for extraction of first food. Then it goes into the upper intestines, where an important function takes place in extracting first food for use in building the body kesdjan.

So what we think of as food is not food; it is simply substance which *contains* first being food. We might think that air itself is second being food. But air, too, only *contains* second food which must be extracted. The method for extraction is to pay attention to one's breathing with the full force of one's attention.

In order to extract third being food from impressions, and to add this to our food substances, and bring these into higher and higher gradations, intentional struggle is necessary. Most people do not know how to struggle, nor do they like to struggle. They do not like the sensations which proceed from struggle, they do not like the stress which comes as a result of struggle. In order to use impressions as a shock, one must create struggle between yes-ing and no-ing. Altogether this makes substances for coating the body kesdjan.

C: What would this struggle be while eating?

G: To know the source of one's food. To recognize those
around one. To see where one is. To receive the impressions
of the food itself, the temperature of the food, the different
tastes of the food. To sense the specific parts of the food
which are entering, including all the spices. All of these
things can be sensed. Not of course to ask one's host what is
in the food or to ask the cook what is in the food. But to, by
taste, separate the components of the food. And also by
texture to separate the components. Every spice has its own
texture, as well as the major texture of the food.

   To also sense the impressions which result from the food's
interaction with the palate, and with the tongue, with the
back of the tongue, and with the throat. To sense inwardly,
that is to say, to gain the impressions that result from the
passage of the food through the body and the interaction of
the glands and the interaction of the organs as they process
the food and extract from it first being food. The smell of the
food and all its gradations. You can also receive the
impressions of the emotional states of those around you, as
they eat the same food, and as they process the food also.
Watch the emanations resulting in them from the ingestion
of this food and from the interaction between themselves as
they sit there. Even if silently, there are reactions which
occur between them. Also one can remember those who do
not presently have the possibility for obtaining food at all.

   There is as well impression of the exact gradations of light.
Light never remains the same during the day, even if
artificially produced. Sound also proceeds during the meal.
For now these impressions will be enough.

S: Is the yes and no struggle experienced in the emotional
center as a result of these impressions?

G: Does that make struggle?

S;   A little bit.

G: Where does it resonate?

S: In my emotional.

G: This is because your thinking center is attached to your emotions. You pass each thought through the emotions to see whether it likes or dislikes.

S: Vice versa, too.

G: Yes. You take in impressions also through the emotional center, and it attaches like and dislike. But this is not what I mean. The struggle between yes and no lasts much longer. If immediately yes or immediately no, no struggle can take place. You, of course, like to end struggle quickly, and you do not like to make a scene inside. So you quickly quiet all parties. You have bouncer inside, that kicks out anyone who makes big fuss. Better to have bar-room brawl every day inside your head, especially when digesting food. The head, you know, is the center of gravity of the personality. You see that? The intellectual center.

S: Not completely, I can accept it.

G: The moving center is the center of gravity of the body. The emotional center is the center of gravity of the essence. Maybe this surprises you.

B: You mentioned that you take a thought and have the thought go right through your emotions. Does that mean that our false emotional center, our mental or intellectual center, runs it through? Basically it is not really run through the emotional center, it is run through the false emotional center that the mind has already set up?

G: Do not confuse yourself. The only emotional center you can know right now is the one you have. How can you know more? More for you right now is a dream. First every experience is filtered through perception. Then from perception it travels through emotional center. And to the impression is attached like or dislike, good or bad. Ordinarily, if the emotional center is healthy and genuine, there is no good or bad. There is no like or dislike. Just as in sex center, there is no good and bad, no like and dislike, no pleasure and pain. In the sex center if it functions correctly, either yes or indifferent. The function of the emotional center is not to say yes and no, but this is what it is used for, ordinarily. Then the impression passes to the intellectual center. There it splits in two. It then goes into storage as memory, and a recording is made along with the tag yes, no, like, dislike, put on it by the emotional center. A memo is sent at this time to the formatory apparatus, which responds in such and such a way according to its own needs. But the memo has to be translated by the formatory apparatus, and the language of each center is different. The formatory apparatus, when she receives the memo first types the memo then translates it into a cliche, and in cliche form passes this on to moving and instinctive center, who translates cliches in a completely different way than either formatory or intellectual center intended. As long as this business scheme of theirs continues, impressions cannot properly be received.

R: So it is the connections. That is what you were talking about with the different centers having to be aligned, last night, and when you say they use a different language. In other words if they are aligned, then they are using the same language?

G: Yes. If they are aligned, they speak a special new language, the inner language of Work. They all learn language of esoteric or mesoteric circle. When first aligned, they learn mesoteric language. By subordinating to Work, centers align somewhat. Then when genuine connection occurs, they all speak esoteric language. By virtue of this, you become member of inner circle of humanity. Then are able to recognize anyone who has done the same thing. Not all at once in the beginning, but eventually. Then you can speak this language together, in outer world.

B: About the shock point with the digestion of the food. Is that, in a sense, an inner language with the....

G: No, no, no. But by trying to accomplish that work, you introduce inadvertently the centers to one another. By making them work together in this way, you at least get them to stop fighting. If only for a moment. Do not forget that they are business partners. Every one of these business partners attends to his own interests. He cares nothing for the interest of his partners, he only cares that they fulfill their function. And the formatory apparatus, which is secretary to all these businessmen, care nothing for the business. And so far from helping them, simply uses prearranged messages. She has a system whereby she does not even have to type. All she need do is send cliches. She prefers to do this so she can polish her nails all day.

B: Those cliches would be habits or associations?

G: Just cliches. Slogan cliches.

J: What would be the nature of the formatory apparatus if she were not polishing her nails?

G: Then she would be fixing her hair.

J: That is all she can do, in other words.

G: It is not all she can do. But it is what she wishes to do more than anything. Very seldom do any of the bosses pay attention. They care nothing for what she does. They very seldom come out of their office, and when they do they do not look to see what she is doing. They are interested in something quite different.

M: So we can use mealtime as a special type of work space for utilizing these three types of food?

G: At the dining table more can be learned than anywhere else. Of course you must not show other groups your function as a group. You must appear to be strangers, you must appear only casually interested in my ideas. I tell you why this is. Maybe some become greedy, not wish to publish third series. Instead publish perhaps false third series; hold genuine third series as "special attraction". This could happen if pupils become center of gravity of a school. I know that without fail within two generations, organization will inevitably happen. I make special provision if somehow a false third series is released.

   In this way I make the assurance my obligations are fully met, and I need not manifest again in this same way in order to meet these obligations of mine.

D: Can other activities in the day, other than at meal times be used for assimilation of second and third being food through conscious breathing and intentional struggle?

G: If first being food is not being processed, then other two activities are useless for that purpose. To practice, not bad. Only cow can chew cud. Other times are more important for other things. Do not become crystallized in desire to make body kesdjan. Other things also are necessary. For instance, if you become completely identified with body kesdjan and its completion, maybe you forget obligation.

R: Are higher being bodies necessary, in order to be able to assist in alleviating the suffering of God?

G: How else? If you are not there to do, how can you do? You must not only be able *to do*, you must also *be*.

M: You said that it was painful to take on new postures. Why is it painful?

G: Humiliation causes pain, *hein*?

M: Why does it cause pain, and what relation does taking on a new posture have with going into a new octave?

G: These are really many questions. First you see if pain is result of humiliation. If true, then you can know for yourself why. Then you are able to see in relation to octave. Everything depends upon making self-effort.

M: You spoke of those in the Work as "fallen angels".

G: At a certain time in one's work, one can go in two directions. Work can become personal, for self, or work can be for big scale.

S: What is the determining factor for choosing the small or the large scale?

G: You wish just to make conversation?

M: Earlier you said that there were specific instructions for this group in regard to your writings. At this time is it also your wish that we make efforts to interest people in your work?

G: Not at all. Your task is to insure that my obligation is fulfilled, and that all three complete series of my ideas become available. Particularly these ideas which I now present to you.

This group is for me *safety factor.* Like nature, I take no risks in this respect. Failure of my own obligation, this risk I dare not take. All I wish now is to make soldiers to fight for new world. I have little hope for present groups. If you wish to avoid mistakes, then work, especially without need for my initiation. Do not make me drive you the way I must drive turkeys to work. Americans have great drive, but no conscience. Americans live for the dollar. They have drive to achieve more, to succeed more, to be biggest on block, but they have not developed conscience; therefore no drive to help God.

Make obligation center of gravity. Then scale of work much bigger than you. You are little. I also am little. But little as we are, we can be big if we remember "magnifier" of obligation. Obligation create necessitiness for being. Obligation makes necessary to *be.* To be in Work one must have ableness. Striving to take obligation is the big inner secret of the fourth way. This I call *Haida yoga.* Haida yogi know something no other yogi knows. He attaches himself to obligation. This is genuine cunning. Because he does this, works for one month when ordinary yogi will work for many lives to accomplish the same thing. Ordinary yogi attaches himself to God for *self*, not for *God.*

C: What preparatory work is necessary to be able to take obligation?

G: Nothing for everyone. For everyone, only ideas.

You never ask what happens to remainder of food, after first, second, and third being foods have been removed.

C: Does it become shit?

G: Becomes *three kinds* of shit. Scientists only know of one kind of shit. There also is shit from air, and from impressions. These are unwanted remainder of these foods. First food shit is released in ordinary toilet. Remainder of second food shit released through "special" toilet. For this one must find very clean "toilet". This special shit can be removed through sex. Not sex for mutual masturbation, but genuine sex for two reasons; to coat higher body, and also make second type of shit useful for nature. Third type of shit excreted through speech. Psychologists know nothing of this. Shit of impressions must be excreted. If not, then head-brain becomes with results of impressions constipated. Those who speak little have shit in head.

W: Are some substances better sources than other substances for particular being food?

G: Substances contained in air are always present in atmosphere. Maybe you like air of Himalayas more than air of sewage. Second food in all air, first food in all food, no matter what. Then is preference according to type. This has already become for you a passion, otherwise, you would not ask. This relates to another, very important idea, the idea of longevity, a most important aim for man.

The divine body of man; its possibilities and manifestations according to law

Ordinary man has no soul. Only in the course of life is it possible for him to acquire a soul. A soul is a great luxury beyond what is provided by nature and is possible only for a few. For all ordinary manifestations a soul is not necessary.

A soul cannot be born from nothing. It is material as is everything existing, although it is formed of very fine matter. In order to acquire a soul it is first necessary to accumulate the required substance.

In order to accumulate the substance required for the formation of the soul we must know where it originates and how to accumulate a sufficient quantity of it. A soul requires a large amount of these substances. The body only produces a very small quantity of it each day. This substance is generally used up by ordinary manifestations.

We must learn to economize these substances not to waste on trifles. Something of this substance must be left over each day beyond that used for ordinary manifestations.

[124]

If crystals are placed in a fixed amount of water they dissolve — up to a certain point — after which they precipitate at the bottom of the container. This point at which crystals will no longer dissolve in solution is called the point of saturation. So it is with the salts which provide the material for the formation of the soul.

Continually within the human organism substances useable for the formation of the soul are being produced, but if needed for ordinary manifestations they quickly dissolve and are dispersed to different parts of the body.

There must have been formed a quantity sufficient for crystallization in order to form the soul.

The crystallization of these substances takes the same form as the physical body but may be separated from it.

There are many categories of bodies called the soul, but only one can be properly called the soul. All others are only soul in relation to a lower manifestation.

If a man should die before the full crystallization of these substances into a higher scale body then along with the death of the physical body the partially formed higher being body also disintegrates and the parts disperse according to their scale of emanation. Parts which originate planetarily return to the planet. Parts which originate in the atmosphere and come from other planets or from the sun return to the atmosphere from which they were taken through the process of extracting second being food from the air.

Even though duration of life is different for astral body from that of the physical body, it is nevertheless subject to eventual death. Just like the physical body, the astral body must live among corresponding conditions, and like a newborn baby is vulnerable to destruction, to starvation, even, unless it receives an education corresponding to the world within which it lives. It cannot exist independently, and is disintegrated just like the physical body if it cannot derive what it needs from the surrounding world.

The second body of man is only a soul when taken in

relation to the first body of man, the planetary body. In this respect it represents the affirming force if we take the physical body as the denying principle, with the reconciling principle represented by the special magnetic attraction between them. This magnetizing force is not possessed by just anyone, and without it mastery of the physical body by the astral is not possible.

Higher bodies can be developed only after the second body has been formed. A third body can be formed within the second. This is sometimes referred to as the mental body of man. In relation to the second and first bodies this third body will be the active principle and the passive once again will be represented by the physical body but this time with the second body representing the reconciling principle.

Still, this is not the soul in the real meaning of the word soul. When the physical body dies the astral body may disintegrate with it, leaving the mental body existing by itself. Even though it is immortal in a limited sense, it will sooner or later die also.

The complete development for man of the soul can only be accomplished with the crystallization of a fourth body, which alone can be called the soul of man in the real sense of the word. The real soul is immortal within the limits of the solar system and to this body belongs Real Will. It is the master of the carriage, and forms the active principle in relation to all the lower bodies considered as a whole.

Following the death of the physical body these four bodies may become separated and exist apart from one another. It is possible for the astral body to reincarnate accidentally within a physical body more or less identical with that in which it was formed originally, but the mental body is able to consciously choose a form for itself in the physical world if it wishes to do so.

If you wish egoism, make friends with an angel. If you wish a soul, make friends with a devil. A devil does not need to make bargains with another devil because both are on same side.

A devil is willing to give the substance necessary for the formation of a soul because the chances are in his favor that it will not escape his domain. The devil is the moon's representative on earth. He considers the substances manufactured in small quantities in the body which can be used for the formation of the soul as his food. He can eat these "seeds" every day. This does not satisfy him, because the seeds are very small. He can choose to sow his seed taking the chance that it may grow and become larger in quantity. Of course by doing this he also takes the chance of losing this seed — or as our esteemed Mulla Nasser Eddin said, "By throwing yogurt into the lake, it may possibly turn the whole lake into yogurt. What a small risk for so great a result!"

Since so few people are able to complete this aim, he loses very little and has much to gain. He hopes that those who work on developing a soul will eventually become tired of the struggle and allow themselves to drift along in the great river instead of fighting to cross to the other river of evolutionary life.

The battle for souls which occurs between Her Majesty the moon and His Endlessness the Sun-Absolute does not take place in Heaven, but on planets, because only man, and not angels, are possible vessels in which development of Real Souls may take place.

Along with the soul must be developed objective conscience — not just subjective conscience for oneself in relation to everything — Real Will, and sense of Obligation to the Absolute. Without these additional qualities, even an immortal soul will eventually be drawn back to the planetary substance and become food for the moon.

The formation of the second body, "the cradle of the soul," makes use of substances of ascending octaves, while the formation of the soul borrows from descending octaves.

P: How is it possible for us to begin this effort?

G: You must find a way to do as I did. During my stay in
Alexandropol many years ago I met at a Chai-Kana a being
who for a number of inexpressible reasons struck me as
unusual not only for a man but in other indefinable ways. I
had long before this made a serious study of all possible
manifestations of man in many different cultural formations,
and in all my experience never had I seen manifestations
even remotely resembling the manifestations of this
individual.

After spending some time together I managed through
indirect means to uncover his disguise, and in this way
discovered that I had befriended a genuine devil, called in
that part of the world a djinn.

When I made this discovery almost certainly impossible
without certain knowledge I asked him certain questions
important for me for the realization of my great aims in life at
that time, among which was the all-important question of the
formation of the soul.

As a result of this question certain facts became known to
me which would have otherwise passed unnoticed in the
course of any ordinary investigations. Among these facts
gleaned from him was the understanding that in order to
crystallize the substances ordinarily produced in the body, a
very minute amount of special "enabling substance" is
required, in the same way as in the manufacture of yogurt a
small amount of special kind of bacteria is needed. "Why are
you telling me all this?" I asked him. "Because I know you
will use this knowledge if you are in possession of it," he
answered. "So few men would risk the hazards incurred in
the preparation and formation of the soul. For the most part
they simply wish to hear about this and then philosophize
about the possibility for the remainder of their useless
lives."

"But as I understand it, everything you do must, according
to the laws to which you are subject, be done by you in
relation to your own interests." I said to him.

"This is definitely to my interest," he replied, "Without the development of souls my live is without meaning, even if a few souls do manage somehow to escape my influence."

"Would it be worth your while to enable me to do as you do?" I asked him, "knowing that I would for my part do everything in my power to help them escape the influence of your domain?"

"I will think about it and meet you here after I have decided," he said. For two years I returned periodically to that Chai-Kana with the hope to meet him again. At last he appeared once again, giving no explanation or apology for the two years' delay. He agreed at once to make possible for me the special implantation of the enabling substance within people specially prepared for this along with the means necessary to capture and refine it within my second being body.

"Why," I asked, "If the answer was already "yes", as is now obvious, did you force me to wait two years for your response?"

"Because," he replied, "It took two years of waiting for you to be properly prepared to receive knowledge." Shortly after this I allowed two beginning groups to form and began to transmit the materials and data necessary to accomplish this aim.

Notes from a talk on soul

If you wish egoism, make friends with an angel. If you wish formation of a soul, make friends with a devil.

The devil is willing to give us the possibility of a soul because the odds are in his favor that we will not completely develop it. The devil has seeds which are already food for him the way they are. He may sow this seed, taking the chance that they may be lost to him forever. He is willing to take the chance that he may be able to reap fully-grown or almost fully-grown souls. He hopes we will get tired of fighting, and because the work of developing a soul is very difficult, we will give up the struggle and return to the path of involution.

The devil is willing to have souls planted. It does not matter who plants them, even if it is someone who is working towards the development and completion of those souls. The odds are in his favor. Along with the soul we must completely develop Conscience, Will and Obligation — Being-Partkdolg-Duty. If these qualities are not completely developed the soul will be drawn back and become food for the moon.

The formation of the kesdjan body (the cradle of the soul) is an ascending octave. The formation of the soul is a descending octave. The physical body is reconciling.

Third talk on soul

Passive force is the lifting force for new formation of being. If the astral body remains passive, then it pushes all one's special higher substances downward, toward the moon. But if the body and outer world can "be passified", then this will force higher substances upward and result will be active astral body.

If one can send higher substances upward toward astral body, then later it will be possible to send other things upward — eventually even real prayer, which is a cosmic substance when properly produced.

Ordinarily the human organism is an apparatus for the downward transformation of substances coming from higher cosmoses. This occurs naturally just by allowing the body to remain active which is the inevitable result of placing one's center of gravity outside oneself, in people, objects and external influences either flowing toward or away from oneself. One can transform this apparatus into a device for transforming ordinary impressions from the outer world, along with first and second being foods, into material for higher worlds just by replacing the center of gravity innerly, and drawing into oneself all results of life in the outer world.

By reversing the cosmic apparatus for transformation of substances one makes oneself useful in certain higher work for cosmic individuals, who will become aware of one sooner or later should one continue to do this faithfully each day. Even though God cannot be aware of a real man, man can make himself known to higher forces who can use him for their own purposes. In this a wise choosing is essential.

J: What are the ordinary substances that are available that are normally wasted, which we could use in the formation of a soul?

G: What they are is not important for you now. Not to waste them is imortant. One small thing we can do is stop all unnecessary movements. Learn to relax every muscle in the body except the one you are using at that moment. Another way is to under no circumstances whatever express negative manifestations. Become active with inside attention. It is possible to bring the body into a passive state so it can act as a denying force. When the body is active, it is active force, thus the second body cannot form. It makes the second body passive. In order to make the second body active, we first before anything else, must make the physical body passive force. Of course, it wishes to remain active, always and in everything. Real doing can only be accomplished when you have power to make the physical body stop "doing". Only use it as absolutely necessary.

Y: Do negative manifestations include thought?

G: The worst thing is to express self, which of course everyone wishes to do. This is why subjective art is a maleficent factor in formation of a soul.

M: Is there another way, an artificial way of getting more substances?

G: Through suffering, yes. In connection with other things. I only indicate existence to you. To learn how is up to you. There are ways of producing great amounts of this substance, but in order to do this you must use forces in quite a different way. To do this you must be willing to give up your ordinary manifestations completely, at least for a certain time. This must be done under definite direction. In the world today, only a few individuals are capable of giving such direction. It will take you years. You must buy time. In order to buy time you must use all your resources of real cunning. The rapid gathering of "enabling substance" in a completely unusual way, creates the preparation necessary. The money necessary to give time to work must be manufactured by you, not on a printing press, but through the use of manual labor only. In short, this aim must be accomplished with no less than the force of your whole being.

For instance, it would not be correct to borrow money to enable you to do this. You could work during that time, but you would have to allow a great many hours of inner work time and somehow in spare time earn money necessary to maintain existence. As I say, you need at least two, maybe three years, during which almost the whole of your attention is concentrated on that one aim.

S: What about raising a family? How do you do that at the same time?

G: You have to find a way. You must use extra cunning because you cannot now earn a living in an ordinary way. If you are not willing to risk everything you have now for yourself, then why should I risk? One may be quite willing to lose everything in Monte Carlo, but not for this work. In casino, what you may win you can understand. Here, what you may win you can not understand; can only taste.

P: It seems to me that money is particularly important

because it is something that we have made through our own efforts. Would it be possible to risk something else, if there were something else that we had made through our own efforts?

G: For some it is possible to retrieve money made through past efforts. Of course everyone wants to pay with "funny money", and win real money in exchange. To pay casino with counterfeit bills can cost your life. Better to gamble with real money or not at all.

C: This has to be manual labor you are talking about.

G: Some people pay emotional, some people pay physical, some people pay mental. I do not tell you how to pay.

L: How is it possible, when doing heavy physical work, to have the body remain passive?

G: When you are doing manual labor, only use the muscles actually needed. Learn to relax all other muscles, especially the brain. Do not fidget. Only use muscles as necessary.

W: I have a question about which first being food substances are best for the formation of the body kesdjan.

G: Some substances, such as the bones of certain fish, eyes, and brains of certain animals. But you probably would not want to eat them, even though they are the best beginning parts to form higher substances. When eating salmon, the vertebrae should be chewed. Marrow of some bones is very valuable, only at certain times of the year. Smoked salmon is much more valuable than fresh salmon. And it has to be eaten at a very different time of the year. Alcohol is also necessary at certain times. And certain cheeses with certain molds in them. At other times certain liquid preparations are necessary. At other times even the inhalation of certain smoke is necessary. The whole science of extracting the most possible of this substance is available with just a little effort.

But again you need two to three years paid for in advance.

F: It cannot be done quicker?

G: I do not think so.

W: You mean allow yourself two to three years of time to gather information?

G: No, to collect substances necessary. You can do this in ordinary life. It would be harmful to stop everything. But still you need a great many hours in each day to accomplish. You must find a way to earn a livelihood very rapidly.

J: So we have to develop three higher bodies?

G: No. Many more.

J: You mentioned the astral, the mental and the divine bodies.

G: Yes, but even the physical body is soul in relation to dog.

J: But from where we are now there are three.

G: You first develop one higher body, then we talk about more higher. Always want to start as President. To be president you must understand subjective needs of clerk as well as objective needs. Of course, your parents never raise you to be a servant. They can be forgiven for this because they knew what it was to involuntarily serve, and they did not like it. For them to be a servant never led to being a master. To become master you must understand the function of the carriage and its mechanical needs, and know the horse from inside. Also must understand the driver and his needs; all lower nature before mastery. This is why human existence is necessary prior to formation of higher bodies. Otherwise we could start with astral body which is real first body of man. Only he can be a good general, who began as a private. To understand a soldier one must suffer as a soldier. One must know completely the potential of everyone under one's command, subjective and objective.

J: You were talking about the kind of resistance that K. and T. had.

G: You, of course, would be concerned in all this because you have heard all these stories and take them seriously.

J: No, it is not that. I feel like there is some kind of resistance in myself.

G: If fail, then fail. At least die like wolfhound.

Preparation of sacred space

Women can learn to activate space for prayer. Only men can make and direct prayer. Women are denying force for preparation of sacred ground, but men become denying force for prayer. In order to send it upward one must make denying force below. The female passive principle cannot become denying force for prayer, but can become denying force for activation of sacred space. Then the men come in and use already activated space. This is how men and women are separate in their functions. They have completely different functions, but accomplish the same purpose. Neither is more important than the other. Women use certain prayers to prepare the space, and then men send prayers upward. The men are good for sending prayers, the women are good for making the space clean and for activating the space.

Of course the women all wish to do what the men can do, and the men all wish to do what the women can do. It is natural for man to wish to do what he cannot do.

P: Do the women also have the function of closing the work area again?

[137]

G: Yes. It must be cleansed after use. In objective sense, woman's place is in real home. Only in this way can women become women as they ought to be, and men become men as they also ought to be.

Women wish to be liberated from their function, and men wish to be liberated from their function. Each feels that the other has the best part of the bargain. Men and women are two sides of the same coin. I do not want to make it easy for you to accept this.

M: The ninety-nine posts in the Work that you mentioned before, are they male or female?

G: Ninety-nine possible laws under which you could make yourself subject never descend into male and female. Those who attach themselves to those laws can be male or female. There is an equal chance for men and women.

M: Each individual has a chief feature which they possibly might crystallize at some point. Does that have anything to do with being male or female?

G: No. To crystallize idiot is by no means unique to male or female.

V

Talk on longevity

M: You have mentioned a means for prolonging life. Could you tell us exactly what you mean?

G: There is no reason biologically why the machine should not last fifteen hundred or even two thousand years. Any scientist, even of new format, would agree with this in theory. Today scientists and men of medicine cannot imagine why it is that the human body ages so rapidly, and even more confounding to them is the reason why the mind sometimes deteriorates long before the body becomes aged.

It is just this little problem engendered by the mechanical needs of our present day society which is the invisible cause of these phenomena. The centers, which should be tapped slowly and paced according to their lifetime potential, are instead forced through the necessities of the accelerated tempo of contemporary life to unravel much faster than was intended. As you already have been told, each center has only so much material, and when that is used up, the center dies. In this way, man in quotation marks always dies by thirds.

If we know the exact contents and capacities of each

center, keeping in mind that all centers have widely differing amounts of life force and substances which do not empty at the same rate, then we can adjust the flow to the correct tempo to insure a long life. To do this means to make consciously an "all-centers-blending-of-several-mutually-paradoxical-flows-at-once". The ancients understood how to do this better, and a long life of Biblical proportions was not uncommon even as late as the time of Babylon.

M: How can we adjust this flow in ourselves?

G: Due to the mechanical necessities of living in the present age, you cannot. But you can insure that no one center will die before the others, by living a three-center life, in which the force of all centers is used proportionately. Someday perhaps we will even return to the slower tempo of real life and thus bring our longevity back to its expected length. Nowadays man has at the most fifty years to attain perfection. For this same work he would need at least one thousand years. It is a matter of economizing energies.

J: If it takes a thousand years to achieve perfection, how can we do in fifty years what we need a thousand years for?

G: True. If it takes one thousand years and you only have fifty, you begin to see the urgency of the situation. In a thousand years, or in fifty years, you still have the same number of impressions, same number of thoughts, same number of actions, same number of breaths, same number of heartbeats, same number of emotions. Everything is the same number, it is just the acceleration. You can do in fifty years what you can do in one thousand, but your inner life is accelerated, so to do it then you must pay much more attention than you would if you had more time. You have been shown why you need the collected state, why to live a three-centered life, and now I show you why you need attention. These are not things that I decide that you need, but things that are necessary to accomplish a particular aim. To do in fifty years you must experience fifty years as if one thousand.

J: So when you say economize it means to use your impressions?

G: No. To economize means just that. To pull the reins back when the horse runs too fast. To grease the wheels. In town remember that the carriage does not get the shaking it needs to lubricate it; that it was designed for a bumpy road. Everything for you now is smooth, so you have to artificially shake the carriage in order to lubricate it. You hold back in certain things, and other things you make more, so that all centers release at corresponding rates. Every center is not exactly the same. One center should release more, another center less. When all substances are expended in one center, that center dies. If you have been throwing away one center or another, that center is sure to die before the others. There are other problems, but that is the basic problem in longevity. Of course, *yogurt* and *kefir* are also necessary.

R: Does that mean that if you operate primarily from one center you should learn to curtail that and use the other centers?

G: What else could I mean?

J: How can you know how many impressions you have left?

G: You have to learn more about what is inside. If I tell, it does you no good. But if you self-observe, then you can know. Now you have a real reason for self-observing. There is a reason behind it. Only you can know the machine subjectively, at least enough to properly use the organism for an aim. If you do not have an aim, you never have necessity to learn proper use.

R: I have some question regarding what happens when all three centers die at once. I am thinking that death is essentially the only place that ordinary man makes a contribution...

G: For all three centers to die at once is very unusual. It is not a feelable contribution. If a man were able to make possible the death of all three centers at once he would feel organic shame at his death if he did nothing beyond that. You are a doctor, do you see anything unusual about that idea?

R: Actually, no. It seems like sometimes medical science occupies itself with maintaining the organism after one or more of the centers have died.

G: One-center and two-center death is responsible for a large number of so-called illnesses. Each category of illness can be explained by the death of one or another of the centers. The peculiarity is that centers can be recharged, but to do this is a very special thing. This is particularly possible in cases of the result of the death of one center; the result we call cancer. To do this requires the transfer of a great amount of force.

C: You talked about the importance of eating yogurt and kefir, could you say more on that?

G: To work properly, yogurt and kefir must be warmed to room temperature. Also alcohol is necessary.

C: Does the yogurt or the kefir lose any of its effectiveness if fruit is added to it?

G: Everything affects everything else. To balance honey in kefir, also add tahini. Those are assisting factors, but they will not prolong life in themselves. Only use as necessary each center. If not, then do everything as before, but be very quick about evolution. You must catch the time.

R: What is the relationship between what people are calling the quickening of everyday life and this now twenty-fold magnification in terms of speed or evolution? It seems what is being said is that everyday life is speeding up more quickly and there is talk that perhaps within eighty years there will be some kind of an event as a result of this ever more rapid living among ordinary, common people. It seems to me that the twenty-fold magnification is going to have to become more and more.

G: Yes. Bad for us. Worse for children, even worse for grandchildren. But since we cannot go back to primitive savage who live one thousand years, we have to be very *bon-ton* and only live seventy years. Mechanical life makes too many demands. Everything you can do in Work, you can do in life. Even with these conditions it is still possible. But you must accelerate your being to compensate for acceleration in outer life. This means to Work forty-eight hours a day, and if it becomes necessary, jump over your own knees twice.

Do not think you have a great deal of time just because you have twenty or thirty or forty years left. It is not a great deal of time at all. Besides which, right now you do not know if you have used up any of your centers or almost used them up. If you have almost used up one center and you show no promise, it is useless for me to refill with "special blood." Also for old age something can be done using breath, but this I talk about later. Everything has come from somewhere. Help cannot come from nowhere. Special help only comes through necessity. If you take obligation, you have necessity so quickly learn to take obligation. Everything else takes too long so quickly learn to take obligation. Everything else takes too much time. You have only small time allotted possible for your Work. You must take only one thing. Best for you to take one thing which makes everything else. In this generation highly accelerated. Next generation, I do not know what will happen, what will have to be done. I wish for your sake and also for mine that we had one thousand years and that we could slowly transmit, elaborate and master each thing one at a time. But first is necessary you live long enough to master everything. In order to assure this, you must take and be accepted in obligation. To take obligation, first must study all sides of obligation. This takes time, but not so much time as one thousand years. Maybe only five years to study. Maybe only five more to prepare. Maybe additionally five to learn to work. Then after fifteen years can take obligation. This is very fast compared to true mastery over long period of time possible for "ancient savages".

If it is not worth to you fifteen years, then this is not for you. Even so, it means hard work every day. Not wait fourteen years and eleven months and work like hell for one month. Everything I teach has a place. End result is acceptance of obligation. You think to take obligation is a small thing. To take obligation is culmination of human life. Before can take obligation must take ableness. Before ableness, willingness. Before willingness, knowledge. Everything leads to understanding, but understanding is not possible without obligation. Or, could be I lead you astray and we all become "son of divine wind."

V: Kamikaze?

G: In order to work, you must understand that you are dead already. If you think you are alive now, why even bother to work? First must realize complete non-entityness. Then realize complete hopelessness of life as ordinary man lives it. Then realize you are ordinary man. Now you see ordinary man, say, "Oh, poor ordinary man. He dies like dog. Me, I hear about ideas, so *I* not perish like dog. Instead *I am special!*" Only thing special about you is you *know* you die like dog, one step above ordinary man who does not know he dies like dog. To be more than dog takes much work. If you are not willing to give work, not willing to make real preparation, then better you go back quick before seat you used to occupy is taken. Uh-oh! Maybe too late already. Seat you used to occupy is very special kind of seat. Right next to has plug. You pull plug, everything you hope for goes down drain. Now for you only thing left is bathtub. But ordinary man he does not let you shit in bathtub. Even though from toilet seat you slip when try to squat.

E: In killing off the three centers, causing the death of the three centers, are you doing that before or after you run out of the energy they have?

G: No. Each center cannot die until all substances in that center are exhausted.

E: You exhaust them?

G: Eleventh hour strikes, and you become two-centered being. Another center dies you become like worm. Worm is good for planet but no good for God.

B: When you exhaust three centers simultaneously, something occurs that repays your debt to nature.

G: You only incur minimum debt to nature now. You cannot help but pay that. Most men wish nothing more than to pay minimum debt, but because of this they get nothing. Only he who takes more obligation receives more in return. Nature must pay. It would be stupid to repay nature only at the end of life. Better repay now, as quickly as possible, your minimum debt, then pay more, then still more, pretty soon people of the Work notice you. They see you paying more, maybe they take you into Work. To do this you must know how to pay more. This I can teach you. But I only show possibility. If you cannot wash dishes or clean vegetables, then why I teach you to pay back? You think work has glamour, but work is like to clean vegetables. To be drone is much bigger than to be man in quotation marks. Real man can be drone. To be slave one must know how to work. Otherwise one is sold, or one is kept simply for breeding, like queen.

C: I have a question about children who are born into the Work. It is something to do with their contribution, and the acceleration.

G: The children born into the Work, their center of gravity is work community. Those who come into the work, their center of gravity is themselves, not just mentally, but also in instinct. Children born into the work do not have to make transference of their center of gravity to the community; they already have it. But you are forced to make this transference. In terms of acceleration, I do not know what you mean.

C: Neither do I, but there is a question there.

G: Maybe it has nothing to do with longevity.

C: Somehow I suspect it does. I do not know exactly how.

G: Well, you have to ponder it. Let it worry you. Make your hair like mine. This is not the result of shaving. This is result of pondering. Digest now. You already full up to throat.

Second talk on longevity

A human being is like a capacitor, or Leyden jar, for impressions. He can live only so long as the jar does not discharge its contents. The capacitor can store only so much force, and when it reaches its degree of fullness it transfers everything which has built up within it to the Anode-Emptying part.

Within the capacitor is a gas which is conductive only after a certain amount of energy-pressure has accumulated. In the human machine this is represented by the cells and nervous system. All brains operate as Leyden Jars for impressions, and when they have reached their fullest possible capacity they inevitably discharge. The Cathode-Beginning of life forces a flow of impressions to begin to accumulate in the capacitor. The more rapid the flow of impressions the more quickly the accumulator reaches its fullest potential, and accordingly dies. One can know one's "capacitance for impressions" and thus regulate oneself more or less for a longer or shorter lifetime. In this way longevity can be attained.

In my own case, I am forced to use and store impressions more rapidly than I would egoistically choose for myself, but since I am perfecting another type of body, I am not

CAPACITOR FOR IMPRESSIONS

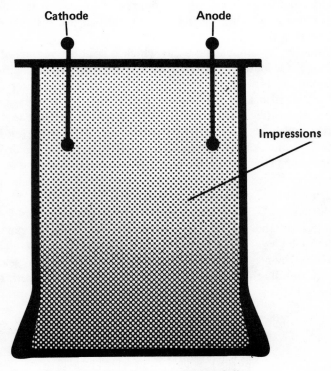

When the accumulator reaches its full
capacitance impressions discharge and
the body dies.

concerned with planetary longevity as most of you should be for the sake of your work on yourselves. At a certain point everyone can feel that their capacitance-fullness has almost been attained, and can, if they are attentive, recognize that their planetary death is near. If necessary, one can isolate himself from impressions more or less and in this way extend his lifetime for several more years should this become for one reason or another imperative.

Laws of world creation and maintenance

During the earliest period of the Universe, only the Sun-Absolute existed, upon which resided God along with His Cherubim and Seraphim. During this time He noted to Himself that the action of Time was directed solely at His world. He decided to provide another food for Time so that it would leave His Own World alone. If He did not take this action, He realized that eventually, even if far in the future, the Sun-Absolute would be completely eaten away.

He decided to isolate Time in such a way that it would exist within everything, but instead of being an absolute, it would become a relative formation of independent arising. In this way it would be contained within matter rather than existing apart from, and continually a threat against, His world.

He was forced to alter the basic laws upon which the Sun-Absolute' operated. Until then the Sun-Absolute required for its existence only one self-sufficient law. This independent force was within itself formed of two other primary laws, the Law of Triads and the Law of Octaves. Our Creator was constrained in order to equalize their actions against one another, to add a third force to these two main laws. This third law is called "Fagolished". It was due to this third force that the self-contained became transformed into depending-on-externals.

The Sun-Absolute had before this time been subject to only two laws of world-maintenance. The first of these laws was the law of threefoldness. This in turn consisted then of three additional sub-laws, called "Holy Affirming", "Holy Denying", and "Holy Rectifying".

The second primary law which had formerly maintained the Sun-Absolute was the Law of Octaves. This consisted of a continual process of involution and evolution proceeding simultaneously within the Sun-Absolute.

This can also be formulated by saying that "a-force-will-constantly-deflect-according-to-law-until-it-ultimately-kisses-its-own-lips."

When the decision was made to alter the laws to which the Sun-Absolute was subject, our creator decided to actualize just those sources from which such external forces and substances could arise, since external matter could not come from nowhere-at-all.

He then re-directed the action of the Law of Triads and Law of Octaves to emanate outward from the Sun-Absolute. Up to that time they had confined themselves within the Sun-Absolute itself. Now the Sun-Absolute began to automatically emanate these Laws, which created corresponding reaction when encountering themselves reflected from the lowest formation of the universal ether.

When these Laws first went into operation, the emanations obtained as a result did not have within themselves the possibility of vivifying all three forces. God was constrained to vivify the third force through His Own Will, creating from the said emanations, through the concentration of His Will, specific fixated points. Later at the said points He gradually began to form — with the help of the said two Laws and also with His Own Will — certain "correspondingnesses". The present results of this action of His can now be seen as Suns which were formed from these earliest concentrations.

Later, following the necessary creations required for the continued automatic existence of the said Suns, these second-formation creations began also to emanate forces from themselves outward, in a manner similar to that function designed by Our Creator for the Sun-Absolute, but on a "Second-Grade Order".

The continued emanations of Second-Grade Forces having thus been guaranteed, it was no longer necessary for God to take active part in further creation. These lower order creations formed automatically due to the continuation of the process of fragmentation simply because by this time both Laws were thoroughly worn out, or "Fagolished", which is to say, they could function only by the action of other forces acting upon them from outside themselves.

From then on the first two basic Laws became cyclic in nature, following the Law of Octaves both within suns and outside them in lower order creations. New suns became relative to each other positive and negative, and relative to them the Sun-Absolute acted as the neutralizing factor for all emanations of new suns. Due to the already established Laws Triads and Octaves, still more fixed points of new format began forming an umbrella, so to speak, around the second-order suns, and upon and within them, because of just these same laws, the "correspondingness" once again formed itself. Now from this activity third-grade suns were formed, thus helping the automatic process of creation to proceed further without the need for direct intervention of Our Creator.

Then because of the action of the major cycle of the Law of Octaves, even smaller formations formed themselves from these down to the smallest possible formation.

The Law of Octaves having completed its major external cycle, continued to evolve and involve within the said smaller cosmoses also.

Later on, these smaller cosmoses functioned for the Universe as machines, just because those two major laws had become "Fagolished".

And so, all substances proceeded automatically to rise and fall on the scale of evolution and involution respectively, from which came the result of transference of substances from one cosmos to another, in which said reciprocal feeding even the Sun-Absolute participated. Because of this, each formation is forced to serve the said process either as food or as a transformer of substances.

Our Creator got the idea to help the evolution for the regulation of these cosmoses. When He first prepared this help for Himself He organized on specific planetary surfaces certain conditions, among which was the possibility that within planetary bodies other bodies could form, but from substances of much higher vibration. These said substances were automatically formed within the atmosphere already existing around the said planetary spheres.

After a while, when astral-bodied beings began functioning on a larger scale, and instinct had already adapted itself for functioning on this scale of obligation, a third body gradually began forming within these second bodies.

The substances necessary for the formation of this third body were results of emanations coming from second-grade suns, which were able to enter solely by means of emanations coming from the Sun-Absolute itself. Only in this third body Soul is it possible to form higher gradations of Reason.

The formation of the second and third bodies of the beings called three-brained arose in this way: After all seven scales of cosmoses had already become machines to pass substances and forces through themselves back and forth on involutionary and evolutionary ladders, so to speak, and began as a result of this to acquire in themselves both high and low vibrations, then according to law, three kinds of substance began forming in bodies of the first type, called "men".

Besides functioning as independent individualities for the formation and transformation of their souls, men also functioned as machines for transformation of substances for all cosmoses. In short, man formed in himself the entire existing reciprocal-feeding process for the Universe.

And since these beings were not only individuals but also cosmoses, they could pass through themselves both evoluting and involuting substances for the process of reciprocal feeding.

Since three kinds of substance resulting from gradations of the major octave are present in and around man's planetary body, the said substances are available for use by them according to their degree of ability to put the said substances to use for their own egoistic aims.

One such substance is that which is formed directly as a result of the radiations of their planet. Another is the result of those substances both emanations and radiations proceeding from their own sun and also from all other planets within their particular solar system. Still another is that matter formed as a result of all emanations coming from every sun in our Universe, among which happens also to be the Sun-Absolute.

We can use as an example of the machine-individuality in which the possibility of a soul has been established, "man". He is made in the image of God — not as he understands it, but in exact similarities.

Everything within him is formed precisely according to the organization and function of the Megalocosmos. He has a head-brain, corresponding in its function exactly to that role played by the Sun-Absolute in relation to the Megalocosmos. His brain cells form the same function as those souls who exist presently on the Sun-Absolute.

He has spinal nodes or fixated points, just as do second-order suns. These said nodes, or fixated points, are resistant to the Law of Triads, just as second-order suns are.

The solar plexus forms a gathering of the nodes of the nervous system, into which all results of powerful impressions resulting from intentional or accidental internal struggle are drawn. And just as the affirming and denying of cosmoses higher and lower clash together, so do the forces passing between the head-brain and the spinal marrow. These struggles result in a neutralizing of their triads, just as all creations of our Universe neutralize the triad forces of the Megalocosmos.

Man uses three different kinds of food for the maintenance and renewal of the sources of each of the three parts of his individuality, each having three different densities of matter.

His first ordinary food is obtained from planetary substances. The second type of food is derived from the air he breathes, which is composed of various substances radiated by both his own planet and by all other planets of his solar system. Along with these substances are also substances derived directly from the emanations of all other suns and even from the direct emanations of the Sun-Absolute. Ordinarily men cannot assimilate these other higher substances because he does not use them consciously. When used in an unconscious way they serve for the continuation of the race and also generally for the maintenance of the common-cosmic harmony of reciprocal maintenance.

Because he does not presently have a real necessity for the conscious assimilation of these higher substances, and also because he does not form in himself the necessity of formation of the vessel of the Soul, he does not understand the use of air other than for ordinary maintenance of the planetary body.

However, man does use these same substances automatically, simply because they enter all bodies to the degree necessary for the continuation of the process of reciprocity. For this unconscious use it is not necessary under any circumstances for anyone to ruffle his self-pampering.

At the present time the conscious use of this second-being food is a complete luxury for man. At one time the use of such food was considered the most important sense of human existence. The process of taking this nourishment was called then "Helping God".

Substances derived from air passing through the nose are also decomposed just as is first-being food. In the lungs this substance is transformed to the next higher octave of the Law of Triads, and becomes "Substances of the Second Octave". These have within themselves all fundamental possibilities of that cosmos, thus are able to mix easily with matter resulting from the transformation of first food into "Third Octave Substances". After mixing they are transformed further into "Fourth-Octave Substances.

Part of these is spent for the maintenance of the machine. The other remaining part, along with other substances forming another more complex mixture, collects in the cerebellum. This resulting substance is called "salt of essence".

One part of this essence-salt is spent for the higher working of the machine. The other remaining part passes through the nerve ganglia, eventually ending up as sperm. In this way they complete themselves to the highest degree possible for automatic evolution of substances. Without the intervention of higher gradations of Reason they cannot proceed further.

Through application of Pure Will for the formation and perfection of the astral body, the substances of sperm are able to be transformed and can pass through to the next highest octave.

The formation and perfection of the said astral body is achieved through the intentional use of these substances from the first, second, and third foods.

When the astral body is perfected, a gradual deposit of still other substances form automatically, as long as life is continually vivifying, and from these salts of higher substances a third body is formed, different in rate of vibration, having different properties and possibilities.

Third-body perfected beings of earlier periods in the

cosmos undertook their obligations in the following way: When their souls had attained the required gradation of reason according to the *Sacred Scale of Reason*, they concluded their business on their planets of arising, completing their existence there, and allowing the planetary body to die.

Then the body of the soul — along with the body of the spirit — separated from the planetary body and rose together to the place from which the substances for the formation of the second body of being originated. They continued their existence in that sphere while perfecting themselves still further. Then they died a second time, in which the body of the soul separated from the body Kesdjan.

The planetary body, having been formed of planetary elements, gradually decomposed into planetary elements. Following the second death of the being, the second body having been formed from substances resulting from the radiations of planets, also decomposed into its original elements, which returned to their gradation of the octave, the solar system.

The body of the soul itself, having been formed of substances resulting from the emanations of suns cannot be decomposed within the solar system. Therefore it becomes immortal within the limits of the solar system. It continues its existence there until its final perfection, and afterward, having attained a specific gradation of reason, becomes a genuine individuality, a unified force in itself, and is no longer subject to exteriorly arising causes.

Following this event these souls were taken to the corresponding place to which their gradations of reason were most suited.

In the planetary body habit is produced by impressions associated and recorded along with sound-senses, or words. On the other hand that same process in the body Kesdjan occurs by means of molecular formations. Cells are formed as permanent recordings directly within the body.

On sacred music

G. told us of another project which occupied him at this time, which was the study of the ancient system of notation called *khazes*. From the earliest manuscripts these "neumes" had been used for the notation of music, especially Sacred Canticles.

In the past few centuries the key to these "neumes" had been forgotten. He has preserved several manuscripts in which eighty-five such signs have been decoded into modern notation. This work is based on work performed by his earliest tutor.

It was in fact for this specific reason that G. frequently visited him. Together, they were able to work out the details of these ancient Sacred Canticles. He said that the manuscripts were in one or another of his trunks or suitcases. In relation to this collaboration, he stated categorically that in spite of his tutor's illness his teacher was responsible for more than three fourths of the work accomplished in this respect, especially his collections of sacred songs and dances.

Their aim then was to place music in general, and ancient music in particular, on a scientific basis, and to make contemporary man aware of the knowledge contained intentionally in such music.

Their renewal of friendship helped formulate plans to publish songbooks for children. Up to that time, G. had been too concentrated on establishing his Work on a large scale to resume work with his tutor as collaborator, but now they were able to discuss such collaboration. They lived only a short distance apart and were able to meet almost every day.

This work would sometimes last past midnight. In all, they notated eighty children's songs. Earlier his tutor had collected similar material, but it had been lost during the period of his exile.

They founded these books on the following principles:

1. Children must have included in their studies both song and dance, since rhythm and movement are vital parts of the life of man.

2. The more refined man's dance and songs, the greater his isolation from nature. They hoped to reverse this effect by the re-introduction of natural rhythms and movements.

3. Religion has lost its previous knowledge of the use of movements and natural rhythms for arousal of religious feelings.

4. Songs and dances should be kept simple, making possible an "all-centers participation".

G. was impressed by the attraction songbooks held for children, not only by the simple essence qualities of the songs, but also by the colorful pictures which invariably accompanied them.

Recognizing the immediate appeal such books would have, he resolved to, as soon as financially possible, publish several such books which would have the effect of bringing his music and dances to public attention not only as a genuine modern legonimism, but also with the added advantage of placing the material "in the hands of beings not yet spoiled by the mechanicality of civilization."

He used as models songbooks published for French and

German schoolchildren. He exercised the greatest possible care in all indications for tempo, nuance, accent and phrasing, so that no mistake would be possible in the performances of these sacred songs. He took pains to notate melodies in exact formation just as they came to him from such *Ashooghs* as "Tjivani". Many of these songs have been used in demonstrations and for music associated with the readings of the first and second series.

He said that he was very careful to preserve intact the natural tempo and interior style of these objective melodies in the process of harmonization. Many of these songs were originally intended as Sacred Canticles for a boys' choir, and were utilized for the purposes of the songbooks as if for a voice with limited range.

Ordinarily these songs were sung without musical instrument accompaniment, but he chose instead to utilize the piano as the best possible means for making them acceptable to European and American audiences. The dances are able through body movement combined with emotional arousing to express objectively true Art. They were originally composed with delicacy, and require mastery not common anywhere outside Central Asia. He did not consider how such dances would be expressed by the gross untrained bodies and voices common to the West.

On his sojourns through the countryside he was often constrained in order to be allowed to notate the music of the area, to join in the dancing and movements, and thus was able to learn all the dances now called "Sacred Temple Dancing", very few of which, actually came from Thibet or Eastern Asia.

With the same regard for choreography as for the accuracy of the musical notation, he developed a method for exact notation of dance.

Peasant songs reflect the natural tempo of life; they may be the solution to counteract the maleficent effects of mechanicality upon the organism of contemporary man.

Perhaps he can regain his harmonious existence through periodic exposure to Objective Sacred Music.

These songs and dances included work, bridal, plowing and drinking songs, and "Songs of exile" which reflect religious feelings, and always have upon the listener the same exact effect regardless of type.

The fundamental difference between these songs and contemporary songs is that ancient songs express objective emotions, not subjective inner expressions of the performer or composer. Along with this, the occupations of the singers and dancers served to form the tempo of these rhythms. In ordinary music of the West, the tempo making the rhythm depends upon suggestibility.

In the beginning, the simplicity of folk songs when contrasted with the richly adorned sacred canticles, puzzled him. After studying these for some time and deriving from each their basic melodic structure, G. discovered that most sacred songs were the same as those sung as secular, but more dressed up in "contemporary bon-ton style". Stripping away the ornamentation, he clearly understood that these simple holiday songs had been dressed in elaborations "just to impart to them solemnity."

He realized soon after beginning this chore of collecting such songs that it was an impossible task to try to save all such songs, particularly exasperating when at the same time the *Ashooghs* were also disappearing forever due to the effects of war, population movement and diseases common to contemporary civilization.

There was an immense task at hand, and he said that it was no exaggeration that he attempted single-handedly what should have required an army of music collectors to do. Along with this, most of his notes were lost or destroyed when he was forced by a series of material disasters to relocate in much smaller quarters.

Index